The Philosophical Reviews of International Politics

Lingkai Kong & Mahmut Akpınar

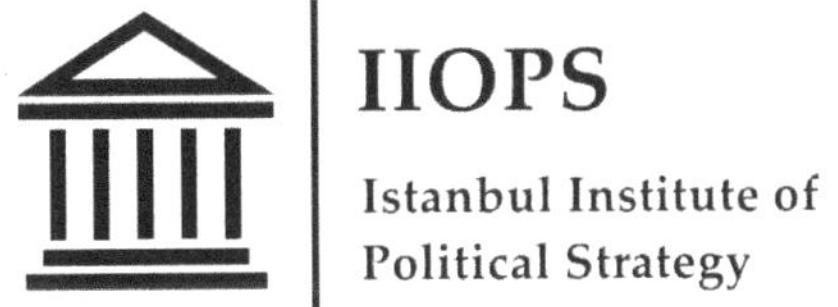

Lingkai Kong & Mahmut Akpınar

Department of Political Science and International Relations

Izmir University of Economics

Izmir, Türkiye

The Philosophical Reviews of International Politics

ISBN: 978-1-7392712-0-6

ISBN: 978-1-7392712-1-3 (eBook)

Type set in Palatino Linotype

Published by Istanbul Institute of Political Strategy

Supported by Istanbul Enstitüsü of Political Strategy Ltd. 219 Kensington High Street, Kensington, London W8 6BD

https://www.istanbul-enstitusu.org/

THE PHILOSOPHICAL REVIEWS OF INTERNATIONAL POLITICS

ACKNOWLEDGEMENT

This book is comprised of 10 chapters in which Lingkai Kong and Mahmut Akpınar examine the following topics in international politics: International Political Theory, Idealism, Realism, Neorealism, Democratic Peace Theory, English School, Social Constructionism, Gender Theme, Marx and Neo-Marxism, and Critical Theory. The 10 chapters are produced and modified partially from the reading reflective essay in the course "International Relation Theories" taught by Dr. Umut Can Adsonmez at the Izmir University of Economics. With the permission of the original authors, we organize and publish the collection of papers.

Due to space limitations, this book cannot be regarded a comprehensive and systematic theoretical investigation; rather, it is a collection of concise reviews. It is not feasible to show all the content of the essential themes in the chosen writings, thus rather than as a comprehensive overview, it would be more suitable to be used as a complement to researchers' expertise in the topic of international political philosophy.

The Istanbul Institute of Political Strategy sponsors and publishes this book.

ABOUT THE AUTHOR

Lingkai Kong

Lingkai Kong gained a Bachelor's degree in Economics from Beijing Foreign Studies University, and a Master's degree in Economics and Quantitative Finance from the University of Zurich, Switzerland. Now he is a PhD candidate in Political Science and International Relations in Izmir University of Economics.

He went to the University of Barcelona in Spain, Solbridge Business School in South Korea for exchange studies, participated in social or academic activities in India, Sri Lanka, USA, and continental Europe. He speaks Chinese, English and Spanish. His research include federalism, democratic theory and he is also interested in the political economy of the Middle East and Turkey. He serves as a reviewer and editorial board member for several journals and runs his own foundation.

Mahmut Akpınar

Mahmut Akpınar graduated from Balıkesir University, Department of International Relations in 2015. He received his master's degree from Dokuz Eylül University in Principles of Ataturk and Turkish Revolution History with thesis titled "Russian Foreign Policy in the Eastern Mediterranean after the Second World War". He continues his PhD education at Izmir University of Economics, Political Science and International Relations doctorate program.

He studied Finance and Management at the University of Finance and Management Bialystok/Poland for one semester with the Erasmus program, and International Relations at the University of Lodz for another semester with the same program. His academic interests include Political History, International Security, European Union, Diplomacy, Conflict Analysis and Resolution.

PREFACE

The system of international political theory is so large and complex that it is difficult for beginners to grasp a map to follow. Thanks to the seminar of Izmir University of Economics and Dr. Umut Can Adsonmez, we were able to have a panoramic view of international political theory and to read and study the most important literature in the field.

After the 4 months of intensive seminar discussions and presentations seminar, Lingkai Kong suggested that we might be able to compile our fascinating discussions into a book to commemorate this meaningful moment. It was also an opportunity to organize our previously fragmented and confusing notes into an ordernalized document. We quickly agreed on the structure and main content of the book and made changes to the previous text. After several months of planning, the book finally came out.

We have compiled 10 reading notes to summarize and comment on some of the important literature in the following areas: Theory of International Politics, Idealism,

Realism, Neorealism, Democratic Peace Theory, English School, Social Constructivism, Gender Theme, Marx and Neo-Marxism, and Critical Theory.

Some of the content is from the face-to-face discussions in the seminar. Due to time constraints and the discrete nature of the material, some of the outstanding discussions were lost and not included in the proceedings, which is a pity. We hope that this short collection of papers will be useful to future learners in their initial understanding of the classic works in the field.

—Mahmut Akpınar, Lingkai Kong
January 31, 2023
Izmir, Türkiye

This page intentionally left blank

For peace.

— Lingkai Kong

CONTENTS

CHAPTER 1

What Is Theory in International Politics ?

Lingkai Kong, Mahmut Akpınar

Introduction

In the first chapter, we will talk about the five works that are listed below: Waltz (1979)'s *Theory of International Politics,* Chernoff (2007)'s *Theory and Metatheory in International Relations: Concepts and Contending Accounts,* Bull (1966)'s *International Theory: The Case for a Classical Approach,* Snidal (2008)'s edition *The Oxford Handbook of International Relations* and Lake (2011)'s *Why "isms" are Evil.* In the initial chapter of his book, Waltz addresses the fundamentals of theory by defining it. Chernoff leads a conversation about typical research methodologies used in the social sciences. Snidal favors the rational choice theory and positivism, whereas Bull advocates for the classical approach and condemns the misuse and ineffectiveness of the scientific approach. Lake makes his appearance at the very end and argues for overcoming differences, celebrating variety, and centering one's attention on particular problems rather than ideology. We manage to strike a balance between summarizing the content and presenting our own unique point of view. On the one hand, it is our obligation to organize and present the reading materials in a manner that is understandable to the reader. On the other hand, we make an effort to prevent this article from being comprised solely of reading notes. As we will explain in the following section of the discourse on empiricism and formalization, it is challenging to find a balance between providing "lossless information" and "touching substantial issues" in a single piece of writing.

The Definition of Theory

In order to avoid being the "young scholar" that Waltz (1979) describes as abusing the term "theory," we first need to comprehend and explain what the theory is. One of the perspectives defines theory as a quantitative collection that does not alter the quality of "laws", whereas laws are a description of the interaction, particularly the causation, of various variables in the real world. When data and indices can be kept as the variables themselves, manipulating the variables and determining the law become much easier. Despite the benefit, this definition has the following three drawbacks that need to be addressed. To begin, in particular practice, multicollinearity difficulties of one variable and another, as well as endogeneity concerns typically manifest themselves. Even if these issues are resolved, the statistical results typically point to a correlational rather than a causal link between the variables. Second, there are a variety of ways in which data may be interpreted and even methods in which it can be altered, and practitioners can employ favorable factors selectively to create rules and to explain theories. Third, the relevance of empiricism is called into further question when it is contrasted with knowledge that is infinite and empirical test cases that are many but finally limited in number.

From a different point of view, theories should not be seen as collections of laws but rather as explanations for those laws (Isaak, 1985). The theories of Aristotle, Galileo, and Newton, which are considered to be among the most influential in the history of the natural sciences, go beyond mere sensory experience and, when combined, serve as an overarching notion. The explanation of law and empirical generalizations, as well as the research that results from new hypotheses, are all major contributors to the power that theory possesses. Einstein suggests that theories are verifiable by experience, but experience does not generate theories but rather laws (Whitaker, 2012). In other words, theory cannot be obtained through induction; in contrast to observable laws, which remain stable over time, theories are subject to change since they are founded on hypotheses that are continually tested or rejected.

This position is supported by Waltz (1979), which comes to the following lyrical and literary conclusion: "Laws remain, theories come and go." Models can also take the form of theories and serve to simplify reality, despite the fact that they may at times be intended to provide comprehensive, all-encompassing explanations. However, the explanatory ability of a model is inversely proportional to the amount of detail it contains (Waltz, 1979; Swinburne, 2010). When a theory attempts to thoroughly build a "mirror reality," it really characterizes rather than explains the phenomenon it seeks to explain. The preceding viewpoint defines theory solely via the lens of law's relative perspective, rather than through the lens of theory itself. If theory is neither a definitive induction of reality nor a set of laws, then what exactly does the term "theory" refer to?

According to Boltzmann (1979 [1905]), a theory is a picture that describes the dominating field as well as its various relationships. Even though it is broken down into fields such as economics, political science, and sociology, the field of research in the social sciences nevertheless demonstrates an enormous degree of complexity and expansion. The theory that is now in the "domain" position may be able to offer general direction inside the field and link other realm parts (Boltzmann, 1979 [1905]). The "picture," although it may appear to be abstract, elucidates both the central idea and its application in a way that does not fundamentally contradict the prior viewpoint that theory functions as an explanation power. In the position of the domain, theory is responsible for making arrangements so that the phenomena may be observed scientifically and hypotheses can be suggested and validated through tests. This ability of theory to give operating direction is reflected in its position as the domain. In contrast to what we stated in the previous paragraph, which was that theory cannot be derived from induction, the theory presented here reconciles the uncertainty of induction and the non-innovation of deduction, thereby achieving the comprehensive optimization of the two in order to construct itself. The three propositions that were just discussed are mutually supportive of one another, and they advance sequentially, contributing to the overall explanation and comprehension of the theory. Waltz (1979) states that "theory is the fundamental goal" (Landau, 1965). Before carrying out research, it is of the utmost importance to adhere to the "proper process of inquiry." After first elaborating on the meaning of the term, we will discuss a number of prevalent hypotheses, in addition to the primary controversy that exists between a scientific and a classical approach.

Naturalists and Anti-naturalists

Whether social sciences may be viewed as analogous to

natural sciences, researchers are divided into naturalists and anti-naturalists factions. The latter comprises hermeneuticists, interpretivists, poststructuralists, and critical theorists, etc. Chernoff (2007) enumerates nine fundamental scientific statements and the most essential concept-causal explanation. The deductive-nomological (d-n) model of explanation presented by Hempel and Oppenheim (1948) and linked to the nine aforementioned statements demonstrates that a particular event (E) occurs when beginning circumstances (C) and universal rules are met (L). In an inductive-statistical (i-s) explanation, the occurrence of event (E) is not certain, but rather plausible. In the early to mid-20th century, logical empiricism had a significant impact alongside the academic paradigm. The objective of logical empiricists is to eliminate interminable philosophical arguments by verification: any proposition that cannot be verified is meaningless. They object to the inclusion of value judgement in research.

Sharing some qualities, logical empiricism and the natural sciences have differing perspectives on causality and establishing theoretical truth. Constructivists and postmodernists are among those who oppose any attempt to apply the natural science technique to social research, as logical empiricism is challenged by other sects. Chernoff (2007) cites eight major empiricist statements and the refutation for each one. Kuhn's new paradigm is an intriguing critique of positivism and empiricism that merits discussion. Kuhn (2012 [1962]) argues that there are different assessment criteria for different theories and that the paradigm is incomparable, not just for social sciences but also for scientific sciences. In addition, he argues that in "immature research" such as social science, there is no universally accepted approach due in part to its sensitivity and complexity.

Among several different hypotheses, we have selected a few representative scholars. Instrumentalists, such as John Dewey (2018 [1948]), think that theory cannot be correct or wrong in and of itself, but should assist us address particular situations. To support Conventionalism and Holism, Duhem (2012 [1906]) exhibits the advancement of study by assessing all features of an item and accepting the physical world's standards. Radical determinationists question whether or not the falsification theory should be abandoned. Scientific realists and empirical scientists debate the validity of established authoritative doctrines. The former accept them, whilst the latter argue that unobservable theoretical things cannot be accepted as true, despite the fact that some theories can be briefly viewed as "basic practical activities" (Chernoff, 2007). While the critical realism is a second critique of empiricism that, still seeking science and causation, embraces and admits unseen social elements.

Classical and Scientific Approaches

The distinction between naturalists and anti-naturalists extends to the technique of classical and scientific methods, as well as empiricism, positivism, and normative, narrative-based approaches. This faction distinction is erroneous and lacks rigor; for instance, the rational choice theory in the scientific method also claims to be normative. However, it does provide a reckless dichotomy of comprehension. We depict the intense dispute between representatives of each party, Bull (1966) and Snidal (2008), assuming they are able to meet, regarding the classical method and rational choice theory in order to investigate how the two impact and promote one another.

Bull contrasts the evolution of two methodologies and acknowledges the developing scientific-approach researchers and their contributions. He provides criteria to demonstrate his neutrality and altruism: the scientific method is not to blame for its rigorous literature or researchers' motivations. Then follows his harsh judgment. First, he argues that the so-called scientific method restricts itself to empirical proofs while avoiding substantive social science questions. Second, a portion of the success of the so-called scientific method rests on the foundation of the classical approach. Third, the technical weaknesses in the scientific method prevent researchers from realizing the original intent: innumerable mistakes and simplifications in the development of data and models diminish the accuracy, such as the difficulty in establishing accurate variables and the discontinuity of the primary actor (substance and preference are changing in the actor-country and society). He emphasizes that data conceals the heterogeneity of individuals and that heterogeneities may cancel one other out, resulting in the loss of knowledge. Fourth, he critiques the arrogance and apathy of certain researchers due to their respect for data. Fifth, he provides examples of scientific work carried out by non-self-proclaimed scientific methodological researchers and demonstrates that rigor and accuracy may also be achieved by the classical method. In the end, he criticizes even the slightest compromise as "eclecticism masquerading as tolerance" (Bull, 1966), and advocates keeping deaf to any voices that adhere to scientific methods.

Before introducing his opponent Snidal's position, it is necessary to point out the logical flaws in Bull's (1966) severe assessment. First, his fear that oversimplification of the data would result in the loss of knowledge and the "cancelling out" of heterogeneities is primarily a technical rather than an ideological issue. To gather data, it is required to exclude or discard useless information. For example, while examining the income of various genders, we will note the individual's "male or female" status, but we don't care if they are left-handed or right-handed. Second, despite the fact that a portion of rigor and precision may be realized through traditional procedures, there is no reason to reject scientific methods. Approach selection does not have to be a black-and-white decision. Lake (2011) characterizes the author's plea to stay deaf to the ambitions of scientific method as typical "crusade" ideology.

If Snidal had the opportunity to hear Bull's appeal immediately, he would be unable to resist the impulse to remain silent. Snidal contrasts the process of rational decision from itself, as the cicada sheds its shell to evade the mantis's pursuit. While acknowledging the limitations of formalization, he contends that his theory integrates universal rules with mathematical models. Modeling is merely one of the rational choice methods, hence criticism of formalization and modeling does not truly damage the rational choice theory. Second, he highlights the adaptability of rational choice theory by arguing that the so-called "constraint" is neither rigid and unchanging: the theory's parameters are adjustable and it may be represented using a soft description. Third, in response to Bull's assertion that certain scientific method success is founded on the outcomes of classical techniques, Snidal asserts that a large number of classical ideas are truly mathematically derived. Both of these are valid, as the evolution of science was initially a spiral process based on the latter's ladder (Engels, 1940). Each can provide several instances to demonstrate that "yours depends on mine," but each example speaks only for itself. Snidal believes that rational choice theory is putting constraints on models, easing criteria for "soft" evidence, and restricting research subject data in order to avoid the rationalization problem as much as possible. Fifth, in response to the criticism that the subject is in a constantly changing situation and cannot be simply measured by data, the rational choice model allows for the changes of the actor or agent, whether it be a country, an enterprise, or an individual, by introducing the *expected utility theory*, which actually adds a parameter to measure the depreciation of the subject's expected gain over time. Snidal (2008) also says that in order to address the issues posed by "preferences, extra actors, and the external institutional environment," the scope and complexity of the theory must extend at the expense of focus and accuracy. Snidal proposes the concept of "effective interests" in order to argue that conventional social science should incorporate certain quantitative techniques in order to seek actual effective goals rather than succumb to naive idealism. His conclusion about formal/empirical approaches providing derivations while soft approaches having the ability to explore a wider field is an typical target criticized by Bull (1966) as "eclecticism".

Embrace Diversity

Ministers constantly propose inclusivity in changes including localization or westernization, just as we see people mediating in street fights. It's time to bring in the nice guy, Lake (2011), who contemplates the damage that religious groups do to scientific inquiry and advocates for accepting and celebrating cultural differences. Scholars should not focus on petty distinctions and build new schools to obtain the status of being "pioneers" (Lake, 2011), but rather on helping people make sense of the world. His label for conventional academic pursuits, "so-called paradigm," reveals his antipathy against dogmatic beliefs. That ironic prefix, "so-called," says a lot. Then he lists a slew of terms ending in "ism," such "Realism," "Liberalism," "Marxism," etc., to make the reader feel queasy. Instead of becoming bogged down in theoretical disputes, he thinks academics should shift their emphasis to concrete problems and experiment with new approaches. The damage done by reifying research categorization is one of his key points. Research efficiency is one of the primary motivations behind creating distinct domains.

Academics should avoid falling into the trap of oversimplified categorization, of mistaking classification for study, and of being unable to integrate across disciplines (Lenin, 1935). Extremism is stoked by the stimulant that reifying provides, and subsequent scholars are inspired to create cults based on a false sense of uniqueness. To make problems worse, academics often cherry-pick which theories to use in order to design studies that support their preexisting hypotheses. At the end, he draws parallels between the sectarian fight for intellectual hegemony and expensive arm races from which no group benefits. Yes, he is absolutely correct. When conducting studies, researchers must draw from a wide variety of techniques. Academics, who like to think of themselves as above the fray, should focus on problem solving rather than ideological crusading; they should strive for consensus rather than conflict; they should maintain ideals rather than be pretentious; and they should prioritize progress over ideological purity. States and political parties do, too, fortunately or unfortunately.

References

Boltzmann, L. (1979). Über die Bedeutung von Theorien. In *Populäre Schriften* (pp. 54–58). Vieweg+Teubner Verlag. https://link.springer.com/chapter/10.1007/978-3-322-86111-5_4

Bull, H. (1966). International theory: The case for a classica l approach. *World Politics, 18*(3), 361–377. https://doi.org/10.2307/2009761

Chernoff, F. (2007). *Theory and metatheory in international relations: Concepts and contending accounts* (2007th ed.). Palgrave Macmillan.

Dewey, J. (2018). *Reconstruction in Philosophy*. Franklin Classics Trade Press.

Duhem, P. M. (2012). *La theorie physique; Son objet, ET SA structure*. General Books.

Engels, F. (1940). *Dialectics of Nature*. International.

Hempel, C. G., & Oppenheim, P. (1948). Studies in the log ic of explanation. *Philosophy of Science, 15*(2), 135–175. https://doi.org/10.1086/286983

Isaak, A. (1985). *Scope and methods of political science* (4th ed.). Wadsworth Publishing.

Kuhn, T. S. (2012). *The structure of scientific revolutions* (50th ed.). University of Chicago Press.

Lake, D. A. (2011). Why "isms" are evil: Theory, epistemology, and academic sects as impediments to understanding and Progress1: Why "isms" are evil. *International Studies Quarterly: A Publication of the International Studies Association, 55*(2), 465–480. https://doi.org/10.1111/j.1468-2478.2011.00661.x

Landau, M. (1965). Due process of inquiry. *The American Be havioral Scientist, 9*(2), 4–10. https://doi.org/10.1177/00027 6426500900202

Lenin, V. I. (1970). *What is to be Done?* (S. V. Utechin & P. Utechin, Trans.). HarperCollins Distribution Services.

Snidal, D., & Reus-Smit, C. (Eds.). (2008). *The Oxford handbook of international relations*. Oxford University Press.

Swinburne, R. (2010). What makes a scientific theory probably true. In *Science and Religion in Dialogue* (pp. 203–212). Wiley-Blackwell.

Waltz, K. N. (1979). *Theory of international politics*. Longman Higher Education.

Whitaker, A. (2012). *Einstein, Bohr and the quantum dilemma: From quantum theory to quantum information* (2nd ed.). Cambridge University Press.

CHAPTER 2

Interwar Idealism

Mahmut Akpınar, Lingkai Kong

Introduction

In the second chapter, we will talk about the five works that are listed below: Osiander (1998)'s *Rereading Early Twentieth Century IR Theory: Idealism Revisited,* Wilson (2003)'s *What is Idealism?* in *The International Theory of Leonard Woolf: A Study in Twentieth-Century Idealism,* Navari (1989)'s *The Great Illusion Revisited: The International Theory of Norman Angell.* Edward Hallett Carr (1946)'s *The Twenty Years' Crisis, 1919-1939,* and Ashworth (2006)'s *Where Are the Idealists in Interwar International Relations?*

Osiander provides criticism for Carr's idealism and additional interpretations, Wilson gives support for Carr's ideas, and Navari provides an analysis of the benefits and drawbacks of The Great Illusion. We will give the audience a complete and all-encompassing understanding by demonstrating how renowned academics have explained and criticized idealism. We will discuss how the historical events led to the development of this concept by painting a picture of how idealism was conceived during the interwar period.

What is Idealism?

Idealism is derived from the Greek word "idea," which is where the phrase "idealism" originated. Plato, a thinker from ancient Greece, is considered the father of idealism. Plato argues that being is an idea, while actual reality is a view. Below what is seen in the world, there are immortal beginnings, which serve as their primary point of departure. There are two primary schools of thought within idealism: the subjective school and the objective school. In the understanding of subjective idealism, the existence is the result of human cognition; while in objective idealism, the existence is the result of a universal concept independent of what humans perceive.

At its most fundamental level, idealism may be seen as an approach to international politics that prioritizes the achievement of specific moral objectives or ideals, in order to make the world a more peaceful or equitable place to live. The absence of a universally accepted definition for the word idealism is, in a significant sense, a direct result of the absence of a universally accepted ontology. On the subject of exactly what type of thing idealism is, there is very little consensus and even very little effort made to arrive at a consensus. Idealism, on the other hand, does not have any unique, independent methods that are supported by assertive lines of reasoning. Wilson (2005), which is generally associated with interwar idealism, and Griffiths (1995), which aims to strip idealism and realism of their rhetorical purposes in order to recover their analytical application, provide the closest resemblance to what we are looking for. Idealism promotes the adoption of alternative strategies for restraining or overcoming the anarchy that exists on the world stage. It is possible that it was most noticeable during the interwar era, although that cannot be determined for certain. Another challenge to overcome is the fact that some writers use phrases like utopian, liberal, liberal internationalist, and even rationalist interchangeably with the term idealist, while other authors hint that there are slight but perhaps significant distinctions between them.

Examples might be helpful when we are making claims about what idealism is or how we can grasp the perspective of it. In his analysis of the socialist movement in 1911, Ramsay MacDonald uses the terms "idealist" and "utopian" to characterize political perspectives that are optimistic and forward-thinking. Woodrow Wilson, the 28th President of the United States, often refers to the idealistic stance adopted by the United States government in its foreign policy as an example of this view of idealism. The inference is that to be an idealist is to strive toward what is feasible in the service of the general good. The use of idealism relates to the fact that it may be used as a general concept rather than a particular model.

Controversy over Idealism

According to Osiander (1998), the idealist school of thought is founded on fallacious premises and, as a result, offered nothing of lasting significance. According to Carr, idealism is presented as a stance that is naive, voluntarist, and progressive, and is founded on overly optimistic and outmoded views of liberal ideology from the nineteenth century, as the basic congruence of the interests of all states or the constructive influence of public opinion. According to this interpretation, another trait of idealism is the disregard for the power question. Osiander makes a comment regarding the idealist ideas made by Hedley Bull where the concepts are identical to those of Car, and attributes to them a self-image in which their responsibility would be to assist this march of progress to overcome the ignorance, the prejudices, the ill will, and the sinister interests that stood in its way. His ideas include a belief in the perfectibility of the international system in line with democratic ideas and the principles of the League of Nations. According to Hedley Bull, the "distinctive quality" of idealism is a belief in the progression of human society and idealism is the central tenet of the progressive philosophical movement of the 1920s and 1930s, with idealists holding the belief that the system that resulted in the First Global War could be reformed into a structure that was fundamentally more peaceful and fair. According to Wilson (2003), the emergence of this kind of order is responsible for "the awakening of democracy, the creation of the international mind, the creation of the League of Nations, the strengthening of international law, and the good works and teachings of men of peace and enlightenment."

For John Vasquez, one of the distinguishing characteristics of the idealist paradigm is the belief that the issue of war can be solved via the application of reason. This assertion is supported by the conviction that there is a fundamental concordance of interests across states and the presence of a developing global community. In contrast to Bull, Vasquez believes that the core of the paradigm is the Wilsonian thesis that democracy leads to peace while dictatorship leads to war. He supports this view because he believes it best explains the relationship between the two. Both David Long and Peter Wilson point out the fact that idealism is used as a phrase during the interwar era. Wilson believes that it is a inter-war idealism, but argues that it is exceedingly amorphous in form; while according to Long, the predominance of something called idealism in inter-war international theory turns out to be an overstatement of Carr, and is strengthened by subsequent writers who provide explanations that are less than thorough.

According to Trevor Taylor, utopianism, in general, is concerned with the development of an ideal state and, to a lesser degree, how such a policy may be achieved. He underlines that this is the primary focus of idealism / utopianism. He also adds that the concept that there is a universal rule of morality and objective justice that can be discovered via reason is one of the byproducts of the utopian confidence in reason that he advocates. Along with Bull, he presumptively thinks that a widespread idea held by utopians is that the flames of conflict are often fanned by nefarious interests such as the production of armaments.

The idealist style of thought places a great lot of importance on the institutions. Both Vasquez and Knutsen argue that one of the most important prescriptions of idealism is the establishment on a global scale of those institutions that have shown to be successful on a local scale in the fight against violence. Therefore, war may be eradicated if the institutions that foster it are either abolished or subjected to significant structural change. A significant portion of the idealist credo in progress is derived from the assumption that institutions are human constructions, which, once they have been established, have the ability to profoundly impact the mind and behaviors of individuals. The human species does not conform to any one mold, while the realities of existence on the world stage are subject to change, therefore, the institutions have the potential to bring about major change.

> "When President Wilson, on his way to the Peace Conference, was asked by some of his advisers whether he thought his plan of a League of Nations would work, he replied briefly: If it won't work, it must be made to work. Wilson did not mention about how is the system work." (Carr, 1946)

Wilson replies (2003) "Collective security, general disarmament, world federation, and other such schemes are, Carr's asserts, the product of pure theory divorced from practical experience." The majority of Carr's critics fall into one of three categories when discussing his concerns. To begin, utopians don't pay much attention to the facts and the study of cause and effect. Instead, they focus their efforts on the specifics of visionary initiatives that will help them achieve the goals that they have set for themselves. Second, they grossly underestimate the significance of power in international politics, while at the same time overestimating the roles, both real and prospective, of morality, law, public opinion, and other forms of non-material punishment. Third, they fail to understand that their acceptance of universal interests amounts to nothing more than the promotion and support of a specific status quo.

Conclusion

During the two decades of the interwar era, the framework of international relations shifted drastically, notably in British circles, as a result of the quick pace of change that occurred within that environment. In all, there are four main stages: The first, which took place from 1918 to 1924 and was dominated by the hopes and disappointments of the peace accords. During the second time period, which lasted from 1924 through 1931, there was a discernible decrease in appeals from the left for the reform of the League and the peace accords, and there was an increasing determination to work within the confines of the League itself. The third stage, which took place between 1931 and 1936, coincides with the time when the League of Nations presented a workable alternative to the existing international order and the time when it came into conflict with fascism. Finally, from 1936 to 1939, many pro-League writers on foreign affairs changed their stance and began lobbying for rearmament as well as collective defense arrangements in order to isolate Germany. The arguments that took place during the interwar period, particularly in Britain, cannot be comprehended without first appreciating the ways in which a shifting international environment influenced and shaped the debates.

For Ashworth (2006), the notion of idealism does not contribute to our comprehension of the interwar period issue at hand. The several unique ideas that are in conflict with one another that are connected with the word idealism do not meaningfully represent the authors of the interwar period, nor does idealism assist us in comprehending the variety of thinking that was prevalent throughout that time period. The notion of idealism provides individuals who regard themselves to be realists with an unsuccessful other to gleefully compare themselves to in order to draw conclusions about themselves. The time between the wars cannot be described using idealism alone. Idealism is not defined by clear boundaries, it is directing one's attention on the highest benefit. Because of this, the meaning of the phrase might shift depending on the individual and the way they are thinking.

References

Ashworth, L. M. (2006). Where are the idealists in interwar International Relations? *Review of International Studies, 32*(2), 291–308. https://doi.org/10.1017/s0260210506007030

Carr, E. H., & Borchard, E. (1946). The twenty years' crisis, 1919-1939: An introduction to the study of international relations. *The Yale Law Journal, 51*(4), 714. https://doi.org/10.2307/792627

Griffiths, M. (1995). *Realism, Idealism And International Politics*. Routledge.

Navari, C. (1989). The great illusion revisited: the international theory of Norman Angell. *Review of International Studies, 15*(4), 341–358. https://doi.org/10.1017/s0260210500112756

Osiander, A. (1998). Rereading early twentieth-century IR theory: Idealism revisited. *International Studies Quarterly: A Publication of the International Studies Association, 42*(3), 409–432. https://doi.org/10.1111/0020-8833.00090

Terzi, M. (2018). Reconstruction of idealism in theorizing scientifically the discipline of international relations for peace and international security: Idea-realism. *Uluslararası*

Kriz ve Siyaset Araştırmaları Dergisi, *2*(1), 10-40.

Wilson, P. (2005). *The international theory of Leonard Woolf: A study in twentieth-century idealism*. Palgrave Macmillan. https://doi.org/10.1057/9781403973733

CHAPTER 3

Utopianism and Classical Realism

Lingkai Kong, Mahmut Akpınar

Introduction

In the third chapter, we will begin the discussion from the works that are listed below: Edward Hallett Carr (1946)'s *The Twenty Years' Crisis, 1919-1939*, Morgenthau (1945)'s *The Evil of Politics and the Ethics of Evil*, and Guzzini (2004)'s *The Enduring Dilemmas of Realism*. Classical realism is defined in opposition to its descendants, neorealism and structural realism, which in turn are defined in contrast to the notion of idealism or utopianism, giving rise to the concept of realism. To put it another way, academics who are referred to be classical realists do not consider themselves to be "classical," but rather, they are seen as being current in their own day.

Although diplomatic operations were prevalent in European nations in the early 20th century, international affairs did not exist as a widely acknowledged and mature discipline until the war of 1914. The conflict, rather than just allowing international politics to be handled by professional diplomats, piques the public's interest in global affairs by exposing flaws in previously hidden agreements (Carr et al., 1946).

In contrast to natural sciences, social sciences are not free from the influence of the researcher's perspective. Scholars of international relations express, in a variety of ways and for a variety of reasons, their desire to alter society (MacIver, 2022 [1936]). Marx, who is bright but solely destructive, intends to bring down the capitalist system in his portrayal of it (Carr, 1946). At the time, Carr had no idea that his academic career would be so strongly related to Marx and the Soviet Union. Nor did he predict his future socialist philosophy to the level that it would be.

Interwar Utopianism

Utopianism, which provides its own imagined vision of

society during the interwar era, pays little regard to actual facts, ignores the examination of cause and effect, and builds basic rules based on its own worldview (Carr et al., 1946). Carr refers to utopia as a step in the development of political science. The use of the term "stage" offers a glimpse into the author's criticism as well as the potential for additional theorizing built on the utopian foundation. Carr recalls the old rustic idealism of ancient Greece and China, when philosophers such as Plato and Confucius proposed imagined political futures based not on what they saw but on their hopes and dreams. In point of fact, there is room for skepticism about Carr's claim that Plato and Sachs's (1992) ideal society and the separation of social classes in "The Republic" do, in reality, represent his observation and diagnosis of the social problem that existed during that era. In the ancient orient, Confucius' search for "benevolence" and for "restoring the rites of the Zhou Dynasty" represent his desire for the antithesis of the prevailing governmental system with decreasing morals and a tumultuous society (Confucius et al., 2014; Legge, 2000 [1861]). While the economic foundations of contemporary idealism may be traced back to the international commerce that flourished in Western Europe, Adam Smith's political economy, which takes into account practice, is predicated on the concept of universal free trade, which has never been successfully implemented. In the 18th century, the rise of individualism prepares the way for utopianism by making the human conscience the ultimate court of appeal in matters of morality. Bentham (1970 [1789]) puts out the idea that morality may be manufactured to "obtain the greatest pleasure for the greatest number." Utopian socialists like Saint-Simon and Fourier in France and Robert Owen in England promote the establishment of a society in which people of all social classes live together during the 19th century industrial revolution in Europe (Carr et al., 1946). All of these forerunners, together with their respective social truths, create the foundations of utopianism in political science, political economics, and socialism, respectively, and lead, after a catastrophic war, to the practice of the League of Nations.

On the other hand, the approach is seen as a failure due to the fact that it was helpless to prevent the Japanese war of aggression in 1931 and the Italian invasion of Ethiopia in 1934. As Carr (1946) puts it: "The course of events after 1931 clearly revealed the inadequacy of pure aspiration as the basis for a science of international politics, and made it possible for the first time to embark on serious critical and analytical thought about international problems."

The apotheosis of public opinion, which holds that public opinion is always correct and will win in the long run, is something that Wilson strongly endorses. This holds the League of Nations back and ultimately leads to a tragic consequence. Utopians are shown to be flawed because of their inability to respond to unexpected occurrences, as well as the fact that they base their solutions on questions of public opinion, morality, and justice. The concept of maximizing individual interests while simultaneously satisfying societal and community interests is known as "harmony of interests," and it can be traced all the way back to Adam Smith's laissez-faire school of thought (Smith, 2015 [1799]). However, throughout particular time periods in history, the remark is understood to be the monopolist's justification for defending their entrenched interests. The notion of social Darwinism has gradually morphed into an imperceptibly changed revisionist model of the harmony of interests, and it conceals a latent potential for imperialist expansion and global war. That is, people and countries pursue their own interests, which are justified by the so-called social harmony of interests, even if it means doing so at the cost of those who are less powerful. Because of the international economic harmony, or, to put it another way, the cooperation of international economies, some industrialized powers are able to ignore the intricate structure of the cultures and economies of other countries, and as a result, they are able to ignore the challenges posed by countries' unequal benefits. The wealth of utopianism conceals the truth that there is an imbalance and unhappiness.

The Development of Realism and Its Dilemmas

The utopianism endeavor that was underway at the time World War II ended up failing due to the aforementioned difficult international issues. The discipline of political science sees the introduction of realism as an alternative hypothesis. Realists explain political theory not from a priori principles (Carr et al., 1946), but rather from history, taking into consideration the structure and condition of interests and power. Machiavelli (2004 [1571]) is credited with popularizing the idea that morality and politics should be kept apart, and the three principles he outlines go on to form the foundation of realism. To begin, events in the past do not occur in a linear fashion. Second, the application of theory does not produce theory. Third, morality is not a function of politics; rather, politics is a function of morality. Hobbes (2018 [1651]) brings together the new doctrine and natural law, and his notion of the anarchy of the state makes a significant contribution to the development of realism. According to the assertion made by Lenin (2017 [1924]), realists believe that political science has its own logic, which is independent of human prescriptions. Marx and his co-authors believe that history is heading inexorably toward one certain conclusion. Because it focuses on the investigation of connections between causes and effects, realism downplays the significance of aims and emphasizes the irrevocable and unavoidable occurrences that take place regardless of the actions of individuals.

The difference between utopianism and realism, according to Sorel (2010 [1887]), is whether the policy changes to adapt to the reality or if the world changes to adapt to the policy. The book by Carr et al. (1946) describes the juxtaposition of the two ideas in a number of different ways. Utopians, for instance, are said to be concerned with the future and illusion, whilst realists are seen to be focused on history and the past. This may be seen as an illustration of the contradiction between free will and determination. The utopians see theory as the guiding principles that political science should adhere to, but the realists view theory as a codification of political practice. This dichotomy between theory and practice is known as the theory-practice gap. Realists perceive the purpose as the result of other facts by disregarding the free will of the purpose, or, to use Carr's words, by recognizing "mechanical principles of causality." Utopians consider the purpose as the ultimate reality; realists see the purpose as the product of other facts. The similarities between a priori and empirical arguments of intellectuals and bureaucrats are derived from this comparison. The League of Nations might be considered as a result of intellect that lacks action, while the bureaucratic method concentrates on finding solutions to individual situations rather than looking for general examples. A connection may also be made between the antithesis and left and right. The first option is considered extreme, and although it is powerful in principle, it is not very effective in reality. The latter is a notion that is deemed to be conservative and feeble. The last antithesis is a debate of ethics and politics, with realists holding the world of nature and utopians holding the world of value as their respective spheres of influence. The former is that politics should adhere to a predetermined set of moral principles. The latter-realists are of the opinion that there is no such thing as a universal morality, and that ethics need to be defined roughly in terms of politics (Carr et al., 1946).

In his book *Ethics and Politics*, Morgenthau (1945) presents a detailed perspective on the subject. He is aware that politics utilizes individuals as a means, which is one of the ways in which politics might be seen as having a potentially wicked quality. While he is arguing that this assumption depends on the superiority of the morality of the individual over the morality of the community, it is important to note that this premise is based on an important distinction. He claims that an individual's morality and a politician's morals are not the same thing and that there is a gap between the two. Even when someone is inspired by good thoughts, their action may turn out to be bad since their goal may surpass their capacity to fulfill it. This is an example of how morality does not totally determine one's behavior. According to Morgenthau, neither science nor anything else can regulate the contradiction that exists between politics and morality, and it is not necessary to condemn political behavior on the basis of moral principles. Political wisdom entails having the ability to skillfully act, that is, in accordance with the norms of the political art. It takes a strong moral character to be able to act politically despite the knowledge that one's actions would always have negative consequences. It takes moral judgment to choose which of numerous expedient acts will result in the least amount of harm. When combined, political intelligence, moral bravery, and moral judgment allow man to find peace with both the political aspect of his existence and the moral destiny that he was born into (Morgenthau, 1945).

Carr et al. (1946) reach their conclusion by proposing a middle ground between realists and utopians by merging the concepts of purpose and cause. The total utopian would deny the existence of a causal sequence as well as the potential of comprehending reality, while the complete realism is someone who has unwavering faith in the existence of a causal sequence but denies the possibility of altering reality for themselves. He is particularly critical of consistent realism due to the fact that it accepts all historical processes and moral judgement, views current facts as inevitable circumstances, and does not provide a firm and meaningful basis.

> "Consistent realism excludes four things which appear to be essential ingredients of all effective

> political thinking: a finite goal, an emotional appeal, a right of moral judgment and a ground for action." (Carr et al., 1946)

The "identity" or "determinacy/distinctiveness" issue and the "conservative" or "justification/tradition" dilemma are both analyzed in Guzzini's (2004) work on realism. The struggle that exists between uniqueness and determinacy is the first problem that has to be solved. When it comes to the interpretation of fundamental ideas in international relations, realists depend on explanations that are not empirical. The unfathomable nature of power makes it the single most significant component of reality. Realists may be able to strengthen their explanations by loosening their materialist assumptions, by abandoning the micro-macro connection, and by utilizing alternative qualitative methods to describe power; yet, by doing so, they risk losing their uniqueness, which is necessary for achieving determinacy. The second problem is the predicament of conservatives. If proof and justification of realism are required in terms of tradition, then realists will need to borrow and update the sociocultural knowledge that is shared by other fields. However, doing so will cause them to lose their academic credibility and cause the discipline to become more conglomerate. When realists apply scientific and concrete logical reasoning, realism diverges from its uniqueness and loses its practical essence.

Guzzini (2004) suggests that there is no need to completely defend realism and that one should accept its flawed continual evolution as well as its failure as an explanatory theory. He argues that this is the case because there is no need to fully defend realism. It is time for realism to break free of its antagonism to utopianism and become more open to addressing the challenges presented by a variety of perspectives. A field of study and its associated theory both contribute to the conditions that eventually lead to the field's extinction. Because of this, "what the bourgeoisie generates, above all, are its own grave-diggers" (Marx and Engels, 2016 [1848]). Realism originates as an alternative to utopianism, yet this antagonism generates the present issue. Nothing is ever made with the intention of being static and unchanging. In his poem *Orchid Pavilion Preface*, which was written in the fourth century, the Chinese poet Wang Xizhi said, "The future generations will reflect upon us, just as we look upon our past." Carr (1946) see utopianism as a "stage," but he does not forecast that it is now time for classical realism to become another stage, where new ideas bloom on its remnants.

References

Bentham, J. (1970). An Introduction to the Principles of Morals and Legislation (1789), ed. by J. *H Burns and HLA Hart, London*.

Carr, E. H. & Borchard, E., (1946). The twenty years' crisis, 1919-1939: An introduction to the study of internation al relations. *The Yale Law Journal*, *51*(4), 714. https://doi.org/10.2307/792627

Confucius. (2014). *The Analects*. Penguin Classics.

Engels, F., & Marx, K. (2015). *The communist manifesto*. Penguin Classics.

Guzzini, S. (2004). The enduring dilemmas of realism in in ternational relations. *European Journal of International Rel ations*, *10*(4), 533–568. https://doi.org/10.1177/1354066104047848

Hobbes, T. (2018). *Leviathan; Or, the matter, form and power of a commonwealth, ecclesiastical and civil*. Franklin Classics.

Legge, J. (2000). *Confucian Analects - the great learning of the doctrine of the mean: Chinese classics*. SMC Publishing.

Lenin, V. I. (2017). *Collected Works: Volume 1*. Verso Books.

Machiavelli, N. (2004). *Le prince*. Ebookslib.

Maciver, R. M. (2022). *Community, A sociological study: Being an attempt to set out the nature and fundamental laws of social life*. Routledge.

Marx, K., & Engels, F. (2016). *Capital: A critical analysis of capitalist production*. Wentworth Press.

Morgenthau, H. J. (1945). The evil of politics and the ethics of evil. *Ethics, 56*(1), 1–18. https://doi.org/10.1086/290471

Plato. (1992). *The Republic*. Everyman's Library.

Smith, A. (2015). *An inquiry into the nature and causes of the wealth of nations*. PergamonMedia.

Sorel, A., Plon, P. E., & Plon, E. (2010). *L'Europe ET la revolution francaise*. BiblioLife.

Woodward, E. L. (1934). Karl Marx: A Study in Fanaticis m. *International Affairs, 13*(5), 721, https://doi.org/10.2307/2602923

CHAPTER 4

Neo-Realism and Hegemonic Stability

Mahmut Akpınar, Lingkai Kong

Introduction

In the forth chapter, we will begin the discussion from the works that are listed below: Keohane (1984)'s *After Hegemony: Cooperation and Discord in the World Political Economy*, Moravcsik (1997)'s *Taking Preferences Seriously: A Liberal Theory of International Politics*, and Waltz (1990)'s *Realist Thought and Neorealist Theory*. Mentioning certain remarks on neorealism and hegemonic stability will be the focus of this chapter.

Neorealism

The conventional theories of international relations based

on the delicate balance of power gave rise to neorealism in the 20th century. The central proposition of this school of thought is that in international politics, the outbreak of war may occur at any given moment. Many people have the impression that the international system is completely and constantly chaotic. Norms, laws and institutions, ideologies, and other elements are all regarded as having an influence on the conduct of individual countries; yet, neorealists often emphasize that these factors do not replace the essential role that conflict plays in international politics. The logic of the system has not been altered, despite the fact that changing state structures have occurred throughout history. According to this theory, one should focus on the way in which international structure, which in this context refers to the distribution of capabilities, particularly among the main countries, influences the results.

The most fundamental tenet of either structural realism or neorealism is the proposition that an explanation for the actions of states can be deduced from the characteristics of the system encompassing those states. Kenneth Waltz (1990) identifies two primary aspects of a state's institutional make-up that serve as structural determinants. He asserts that all state systems are comparable in that their organizational structures are anarchic rather than hierarchical. Nevertheless, there are also fundamental disparities amongst anarchic systems because of variations in the allocation of power among the component states. One of the concerns that emerges about the characteristics of all different kinds of systems that have an anarchic structure is the debate that takes place between defensive realists and aggressive realists.

The realist views the world as consisting of several states that interact with one another, while neorealists believe that the only way to study interacting states in an effective manner is to differentiate between structural causes and effects and unit-level causes and effects. Both as a fresh subject of investigation and as a status for debate, structure emerges as an important factor. Realists like Aron, Morgenthau, and others sought to comprehend and explain the results of international events by evaluating the actions and interactions of the many components, including the nations that occupy the international arena and the individuals who steer the policies of those governments. The technique that traditional realists use is essentially inductive, while the logical process is emphasized more in neorealism.

In contrast to the old realism, the new realism first proposes a solution to the problem of distinguishing between factors internal to international political systems and those that are external to those systems. Neorealism proves the autonomy of international politics and, as a result, makes it feasible to develop a theory about it, by proving an international political system as a whole, with structural and unit levels that are both different and related. The notion of a system's structure is developed further by neorealism, which allows people to perceive how the structure of a system, as well as modifications in it, affects the interacting units and the results they create. The interaction of nations is what gives rise to the formation of international structure, which subsequently prevents states from engaging in some behaviors. The organizing principle of the system, which in this case is anarchy, and the distribution of capabilities across different units are two characteristics that are used to identify different types of international systems. Structures in an anarchic field are often characterized by the tens of their most important components. When there are fewer or more major powers, the composition of international systems changes significantly. The basic difference between traditional realism and neorealist theory is that neorealists hold the view that international politics may be conceptualized as a system that has a well-defined structure. Robert Keohane maintains that neorealist theory is amenable to gradual alterations in order to achieve a closer connection with reality.

Neorealism, Bipolarity and Multipolarity System

Before Waltz, the majority of authors who wrote on international politics centered their attention on the topic of whether or not power was allocated evenly or unequally among states. Since Waltz's comment, almost everyone's attention has been focused on the question of whether or not systems are characterised by a multi-polar or a bipolar distribution of power. The concept of bipolarity, as opposed to multipolarity, was developed by Waltz as a result of discussions over how best to comprehend the cold war. After the invention of nuclear weapons, the world's most powerful nations seemed to be dividing themselves into two antagonistic coalitions, which were kept apart by insurmountable ideological divides. This second characteristic of postwar international politics was eventually dubbed "bipolarity" at some point. Waltz believed that a multipolar world was more prone to the outbreak of conflict than a bipolar society.

> "States are less likely to misjudge their relative strengths than they are to misjudge the strength and reliability of opposing coalitions. Rather than making states properly cautious and forwarding the chances of peace, uncertainty and miscalculation cause wars...In a bipolar world uncertainty lessens and calculations are easier to make." (Waltz, 1990)

"A bipolar world is one in which there are two great powers, and a multipolar world is one in which there are more than two great powers." According to Waltz, alliances are significant in a multipolar world but are not significant in a bipolar world. To put this another way, the type of mistakes that lead to conflict are less likely to occur in a bipolar world. The phenomena of anarchy is seen as a cause by neorealists, and they recognize it as an essential beginning point in the process of analyzing the foreign policy of nations. Therefore, according to neorealists who place a strong emphasis on the ideas of "security dilemma" and "self-help," the actions that every state engages in to maintain its security put the security of its existing or prospective opponents at jeopardy. Absolute security for one state equals complete and utter insecurity for all other states, and this condition of affairs compels those other nations to behave in an aggressive manner. The fear that one state will be ruled by others is what dictates the conduct of states, according to neorealism, which explains the behavior of states using anarchy as an explanation. It is not taken into account that fear may emerge from misunderstanding, prejudice, or a lack of knowledge, nor is it taken into account that certain governments may not follow expansionist policies.

One other distinction that can be made between realism and neorealism is with regard to the scientific basis of their respective statements. Statements of neorealism examined in the behavioral response to traditional neorealism, which is connected to human nature, does not have the capability of being tested. It is not conceivable to witness the premises about human nature, according to positivism; hence, it is not viable to accept classical realism as a scientific theory from this point of view. Keohane (2005) defines neorealism as an attempt to make realism a theory of international politics. Neorealism may be seen as an extension of their work. In his criticism of realism and neorealism, Shimko

(1992) states: There is no unavoidable, objective conflict of interest when parties are driven by fear of one other; resolving these worries would provide both with a sense of security. There will always be a conflict of interest when players are driven by the need to dominate one another since it is illogical to think that the needs of all parties involved can be satisfied at the same time. In light of this, classical realism contends that there would always be a conflict of interests between social actors like nation governments, however neorealism does not support this position. In the neorealist formulation, the root of conflict and violence would be eliminated. If one feels secure, there is no motive to control and dominate other people since one does not need to worry about their own safety. It is quite difficult to pinpoint any one cause of the ongoing war and is definitely more hopeful than the traditional realist formulation when it comes to comprehending conflict.

The international liberal theory, in contrast to the realist theory, places more emphasis on international cooperation and peace than it does on international conflict. Liberals need to acknowledge the presence of other players than governments. In contrast to realism, the idea of international liberalism views international institutions as factors that contribute to maintaining peace and security. Another distinction between liberals and realists is the amount of analysis they use. Analyses at the unit level are used by neoliberals, and analyses at the system level are utilized by neorealists.

Hegemonic Cooperation and Stability

The history of hegemonic cooperation encourages reflections on three more fundamental issues in the analysis of international politics: the relationship between power and interdependence, the problem of maintaining hegemony, and the nature of hegemony's connections to international regimes and cooperation. The challenge of preserving hegemony is a further concern. For long-term success, a hegemonic strategy must continually refresh the circumstances for its own survival. Unless a plan generates strength, hegemony will inevitably crumble. Any hegemonic leadership strategy must thus aim to preserve the national resource foundation upon which government authority and leadership rely.

As emphasized by realists, the functioning of international

institutions is contingent upon the allocation and use of power. Nevertheless, if hegemony may replace the functioning of international regimes, then a reduction in hegemony may enhance the need for international regimes. This is by no means a guarantee that international institutions will emerge in response to government demand, but it does imply that, after hegemony, regimes may become potentially more essential as a method of reducing uncertainty and encouraging mutually advantageous accords. When attempting to comprehend how international relations function, neorealism is one of the most applicable theories, since the cause for the international arena's chaotic structure is the system itself, not the character of the individual.

References

Harrison Wagner, R. (2010). *War and the state: The theory of international politics*. University of Michigan Press. htt ps://doi.org/10.3998/mpub.224944

Keohane, R. O. (2005). *After hegemony: Cooperation and discor d in the world political economy*. Princeton University Pr ess.

Moravcsik, A. (1997). Taking preferences seriously: A liber al theory of international politics. *International Organizat ion*, *51*(4), 513–553. https://doi.org/10.1162/002081897550447

Shimko, K. I. (1992). Realism, neorealism, and American li beralism. *The Review of Politics*, *54*(2), 281–301. https://do i.org/10.1017/s0034670500017848

Tayyar, A. R. I. (2013). Uluslararası ilişkiler Teorileri: Çatış ma, Hegemonya, işbirliği. *Baskı, Bursa: MKM Yayıncılık.*

Waltz, K. N. (1990). Realist Thought and Neorealist Theor y. *Journal of International Affairs*, *44*(1), 21.

CHAPTER 5

Liberalism Democratic Peace

Lingkai Kong, Mahmut Akpınar

Introduction

According to the liberal democratic peace theory, a liberal democratic state seldom or never engages in wars with another. This is merely the most simplest form of the theory; in reality, the present theory involves a great deal of definitions and assumptions. We will continue to develop and expand it based on the research of three scholars: Owen (1994)'s *How Liberalism Produces Democratic Peace,* Doyle (2017)'s *Kant, Liberal Legacies, and Foreign Affairs,* and Oneal et al. (2003)'s *Causes of Peace: Democracy, Interdependence, and International Organizations.*

Freedom and Liberalism Democratic Peace

Doyle uses an encyclopedic method to organize the period from 1816 to 1980 spanning the entry of many nations into liberal democracy and the occurrence of world wars. He concludes that liberal nations do not go to war with one another, despite the fact that liberal governments continue to engage in conflict with non-liberal democracies. To clarify this idea, which will be termed "liberal democratic peace" in the future, Doyle (2017) first describes "freedom" and describes two distinct conceptions of liberal democratic governance. Negative freedom is freedom of conscience, a free press and free speech, equality under the law, a freedom that is dictated by the government and does not need individual initiative. Positive freedom is freedom of religion, a free press, and freedom of expression and refers to the quality of educational possibilities and the right to health care and work, which allows and empowers people to enhance their talents and chances. Doyle states that democratic involvement is the foundation for both of the aforementioned liberties. The author contrasts between two approaches to reconciling individual liberty and governmental order. One is laissez-faire or "conservative" liberalism, and the other is social welfare or social democracy, with the former emphasizing the limitation of governmental power to protect individual property and the latter emphasizing that government functions should be expanded to promote individual opportunity and freedom.

To explain liberal democratic peace, Doyle (2017) refutes and illustrates the fragility of the realist theory of balance of power using the examples of Louis XIV, Napoleon, and Hitler. Aron (2017) outlines three forms of interstate peace: empire, hegemony, and equilibrium, which are mentioned by Doyle. The first category, peace inside the empire, does not correspond to the idea of independent liberal peace we are discussing today. The second is the peace of hegemony: using the example of France in the 17th century, the author demonstrates that hegemony does not inevitably produce peace. Regarding equilibrium peace, neither bipolar equilibrium nor multipolar equilibrium have abolished minor power and regional disputes. Doyle (2017) also names additional liberals with insufficient peacekeeping justifications.

Doyle (2017) then references Kant's "perpetual peace" (2005 [1795]). Permanent peace will be assured by the ever-increasing acceptance of three final elements of peace, by the formation of a republican constitution, a broad democratic unity, and a cosmopolitan law. Oneal et al. (2003) states that they are republican constitutions, international organizations, and "cosmopolitan law" that are expressed in free trade and economic interdependence. Once a republican institution is created, the republican tradition of protecting the people's interests will resist an invading war that is destructive to the people's well-being. The international organization of a liberal democracy may assist each other in the face of economic and military challenges, therefore the fall of American hegemony may pose threats to the liberal world (Doyle, 2017). Foreigners are not to be treated with hatred, but with universal hospitality, according to cosmopolitan law, which permits the "spirit of commerce" and encourages the linkage of trade, so helping countries and peoples to avoid expensive conflicts. Doyle (2017) also notes at the conclusion of Kant's *Liberal Legacies, and Foreign Affairs* that although liberal peace does not eliminate security issues, it does lower tensions.

Strategic alliances are not secure, and neither are economic alliances. However, the confidence in a liberal democratic state and the political connection of liberal rights and interests may serve as a foundation for peace and reciprocal nonaggression. The empirical research by Oneal et al. (2003)

that examines liberalism, trade, democratization, and other significant factors substantiates Doyle's plea for liberal democracy. Oneal et al. (2003) find that the likelihood of conflict is decreased by 86% when both sides are liberal democracies. In response to the claim of some academics that democracy in Eastern Europe has caused conflict and turmoil, the authors assert that no such evidence exists. In addition, he thinks that greater U.S.-China economic dependency reduces the likelihood of war considerably. Additionally, the authors evaluate the gravity model, which argues that nation population, size, and distance effect commerce, and that armed conflicts may quickly affect trade. Optimistically, he concludes that while realism now dominates world politics, the Kantian system must be promoted for the sake of global political, economic, and peaceful success.

Mechanism of Democratic Peace and Foreign Policy

If Doyle's paper is an introduction to liberalism democratic peace without specifying a mechanism, and Oneal employs an empirical approach without providing a theoretical explanation, then Owen counters the realists' criticism of liberalism with historical evidence and an interpretivist approach, and provides several important principles of foreign policy of liberal democracies that serve as the causal mechanism for the liberalism democratic peace thesis.

In answer to the question, "What is a democratic state?" Owen (1994) characterizes a liberal democracy as one in which the general populace has influence on war choices. As long as they are free, peace-loving, and educated, it is the people, not a handful of tyrants, who determine whether to wage war. Under other words, in a society with free speech and competitive elections, the democratic institutions have a role in preventing conflict.

Non-democracies seek conquest or pillage, while democracies promote the genuine interests of their people. For illiberal democracies (using ancient Athens as examples), although having the shape of democratic institutions, they do not realize freedom owing to the absence of commonality, respected heroism, etc. This remark is also consistent with the first definition, which asks if the educated and free people has the authority to decide on war. Owen (1994) then discusses the foreign policies of liberal democracies. How do liberal democracies see other democratic and non-democratic nations? Does it fit within the democratic peace framework? When creating foreign policy, the major concern of liberals is whether the opposing side is a liberal democracy. The starting position is fundamentally distinct from that of neorealists, who emphasize state capability first.

Owen (1994) provides several solutions. It is not true that being a liberal democracy itself prevents conflict with another liberal democracy; the perspective of the opposing side is equally significant. Despite possessing an election system and a theoretical liberal democracy, the Weimar Republic was unable to join the democratic peace framework because France and the United States did not see it as liberal. Public mobilization is required for democracies to engage a war, since leaders must persuade the populace that there is a justification and that the other side is a non-democratic state. If not, the people may exert influence and pressure on war policy via liberal opinion expressed in newspapers, radio, and other media in order to reduce the rationale for war.

Owen (1994) outlines six foreign policy fundamentals for liberal democracies. And he utilizes the historical

Franco-American disputes and diplomatic transactions of 1796-98, together with the British and American conflicts of 1803-12, 1861-63, and 1895-96, to demonstrate them. Since the author's original words are so succinct and clear, I adopt them word for word:

> "1. Liberals will trust states they consider liberal and mistrust those they consider illiberal. 2. When liberals observe a foreign state becoming liberal by their own standards, they will expect pacific relations with it. 3. Liberals will claim that fellow liberal democracies share their ends, and that illiberal states do not. 4. Liberals will not change their assessments of foreign states during crises with those states unless those states change their institution. 5. Liberal elites will agitate for their policies during war-threatening crises. 6. During crises, statesmen will be constrained to follow liberal policy." (Owen, 1994)

Owen refutes the criticisms raised by realists to the democratic peace theory, but he does not dismiss their emphasis on power and actual forces. Owen successfully combines realism with liberalism and argues that the key is to identify the national interest in order to collaborate with liberal democracy. He refers to the following two hypotheses and modifies each somewhat and argues that, according to Walt's (2013) balance-of-threat theory, liberal state intentions still depend in part on whether the opposing side is liberal. Owen highlights the contradiction between neorealism and democratic peace on this issue in relation to the second approach, which assumes that international anarchy does not lead to power politics. Despite the immense successes of liberal democratic peace, Owen concludes that eternal peace cannot be taken for granted. First, the material deficiency brought on by peace may make conflict more appealing. Second, liberalism may disrupt traditional ways of life, leading to local instability, hostility, and opposition to democracy. In order to prevent these traps from jeopardizing the fundamental core of free democracy, there is no room for relaxation.

References

Doyle, M. W. (2017). Kant, liberal legacies, and foreign aff airs. In *Immanuel Kant* (pp. 503–533). Routledge.

Kant, I. (2005). *Perpetual Peace* (M. C. Smith, Trans.). Cosim o Classics.

Oneal, J. R., Russett, B., & Berbaum, M. L. (2003). Causes of peace: Democracy, interdependence, and internation al organizations, 1885-1992. *International Studies Quarterl y: A Publication of the International Studies Association, 4 7*(3), 371–393. https://doi.org/10.1111/1468-2478.4703004

Owen, J. M. (1994). How liberalism produces democratic p eace. *International Security, 19*(2), 87. https://doi.org/10.23 07/2539197

Aron, R., & Thompson, P. (2017). *Peace and war: A theory o f international relations*. Routledge.

Thucydides. (1963). *History of the peloponnesian war* (R. Warn er, Trans.). Penguin Classics.

Walt, S. M. (2013). *The origins of alliances*. Cornell Universit y Press.

CHAPTER 6

The English School

Mahmut Akpınar, Lingkai Kong

Introduction

The English School of international relations is the one that has been around the longest and is often considered to be the most significant competitor to the American mainstream. The approach that the English School takes to the study of international relations integrates theory and history as well as ethics, power, and structure. We will continue to develop and expand our discussion based on the research of four scholars: Buzan (2001)'s *The English School: an underexploited resource in IR*, Buzan and Lawson (2017)'s *The English School: History and primary institutions as Empirical IR theory*, Bull (1971)'s *Order vs. Justice in International Society* and Dunne et al. (2020)'s *International Relations Theories: Discipline and Diversity*.

The History of English School

The British Committee on the Theory of International Politics, which first began holding meetings in the late 1950s, is considered to be the origin of the English School. The members of the English School are a group of academics that are mostly based in the United Kingdom, having a similar ontological inclination and are skeptical of the sort of scientific method that is promoted by positivists. The development of the English School may be broken down into four stages:

The first stage, which begins in 1959 with the formation of the British Committee and ends in 1966 with the publishing of Butterfield and Wight's *Diplomatic Investigations,* is considered to be the beginning of this school. During this time, the Committee shifted its attention to place a greater emphasis on international society as the primary focus of its preferred method to theorizing about international relations.

The second stage begins in 1966 and keeps going until 1977,

the year in which two of the foundational texts of the English School were published: Bull's *The Anarchical Society,* which centered on the nature of Western international society, and Wight's *Systems of States,* which opened up the exploration of international society in the context of world history.

The third stage begins in 1977 and lasts until it's completed in 1992. It is primarily about strengthening the English School, and transferring the mantle to a subsequent cohort of students. The activity of the British Committee lasted until the middle of the 1980s; however, with Bull's death, the formal framework of regular meetings began to fall apart, which ultimately led to the conclusion of the British Committee stage of the English School. During this time period, Roy Jones bestowed the name "English School" to the institution he founded.

The forth stage begins in 1992 and continues to the current day. It is about the emergence of a new generation of English School writers who have few or no direct ties to the British Committee and who are more receptive to collaborating with ideas and methods associated with the English School within the broader context of advancements in international relations theory in general.

Throughout these stages, the English School has been successful in reproducing itself both through the force of its ideas that have been passed down through three generations of academics and through the influence of several of its central figures and regular contributors on the graduate students of the school. But from the 1990s it was unable to reestablish the prolonged discussion forums that played such an important part in invigorating and directing the work of previous generations.

The Idea of English School

Wight is credited with establishing the "English School". His interpretation of the nameless English School is recognized as the paradigm's first fully developed theory, which is denoted by the letter "T0". Subsequent iterations of the paradigm are denoted by the letters "T1", "T2", and so on. It is believed that Bull later developed the idea of "T1". The following is a list of the four axioms that have parametric status according to the English School:

> 1. "The primary actors in the international system are sovereign city states or nation-states" 2. "In international relations, there is a 'system of states' whenever two or more states have sufficient contact between them and have sufficient impact on each other's decisions" 3. "There is 'anarchy' in the international system, meaning no common government" 4. "States in the international system exist in an 'international society' in which they recognize the common interests and common values forming a society in the sense that they conceive themselves to be bound by a common set of rules governing relations with one another and share in the working of common institutions." (Bull, 1971)

These axioms with a parametric status provide the solid foundation, in philosophical words, the axioms define the "constitution" of the English School as a research organization. The assumptions of Axioms 1 and 3 inside the hard core of the English School are strikingly similar to those of realism and structural realism. In contrast, axioms 2 and 4 are unique and notably distinguish the English School from other paradigms. The axiom 2 argues that an international system occurs when the states of the actors interact so that each must consider the conduct of the others. Bull puts forward a definition: A system of states shaped "when two or more states have sufficient contact between them, and have sufficient impact on one another decisions to cause them to behave at least in some measure as parts of a whole".

Bull asserts that the international state-system is distinct from the suzerain state system. In suzerain state-systems, a single power dominates the weaker nations that surround it. In the course of history, there have been main and secondary state systems. The primary system consists of sovereign nations, while the secondary system is comprised of systems of states that are often suzerain state systems. In "T0" stage, there is an international society inherent in the relations between nations and that it would be implausible to assume that politicians are motivated only by power and not by notions of right and justice, but with the coexistence of cooperation and conflict in the international system, as shown by diplomacy, international law, and institutions.

"International society" is often connected with the English School of international relations theory, known as the international society approach. It is most often associated with Hedley Bull (1971)'s "Anarchical Society," in which Bull contrasts British methods to international affairs with American and realist views in which nations use power politics and egoistic materialism, with "rules of the jungle" as the sole laws. Bull claims that while the international arena exemplifies anarchy in the absence of a central authority to create and enforce laws, this does not mean that international politics are anarchic or disorderly. In contrast to the "billiard-ball metaphor" of international politics, nations are not just independent parts of a system, but there is a strong institutionalization of shared beliefs, mutual understandings, and similar interests; hence, the term "anarchical society" may be used.

The English School methodology has a number of unique foci. Suganami stresses institutions, whereas Jackson and Buzan (2001) emphasize agents and structures, respectively. They contend that the core ideas of the English curriculum are the international system, international society, and global society. Bull's renowned model of society is based on a sort of structural functionalism which asserts that all human civilizations must be founded on three fundamental interests. First, security against violence: non-intervention, balance of power, conflict, great power management, and human rights. Second, respect for agreements: diplomacy and international law. Third, property rights: territoriality, sovereignty, colonialism, nationalism, and dynasticism.

According to Bull's classical definition, international society emerges when a group of states, conscious of certain shared interests and values, forms a society in the sense that they believe they are bound by a common set of rules in their relations with one another and participate in the operation of shared institutions. The uniqueness of the membership, which is confined to sovereign nations, is the first essential component of international society. An worldwide society's structure begins with its acknowledgment. While the notion of mutual recognition is essential to the English school's conception of international society, it is insufficient as a sufficient prerequisite for its existence. The players must have some shared interests, such as commerce, freedom of movement, or just the desire for stability. However, the independence of sovereign nations continues to be a significant impediment to the achievement of shared objectives.

Pluralist and Solidarist

In a pluralist international society, the institutional structure serves both the liberty of nations and the preservation of order among them. It is sufficient to recall that the English school considered great powers, limited conflict, and the balance of power to be institutions in order to properly comprehend the pluralist order. Pluralism emphasizes that all states have equal rights, regardless of their capabilities or internal structure. Solidarity, according to a solidarist international society, is an expansion of a worldwide society, not its alteration. As with pluralism, it is characterized by common ideals and institutions and kept together by legally enforceable laws. The distinctions lie in the substance of the values and the nature of the laws and institutions.

The pluralist-solidarist schism within the English School is not insurmountable with regard to a significant aspect. Principally, the two sides argue about what is feasible within the present society of all governments. Even pluralists would not dispute that there may be regional groupings of governments within which higher objectives, such as the preservation and safeguarding of human rights, might be achieved successfully. Bull states his views on the advancement of human rights in international affairs and is vehemently opposed of "solidarity." As stated by Bull, solidarities exist in the form of pluralism. Perhaps it is not an exaggeration to state that the majority of English School philosophers are, at heart, solidarists; nevertheless, they may differ on the degree of solidarity they claim to see in the world they study.

References

Bull, H. (1971). *Order vs. justice in international society*. Polit ical Studies, *19*(3), 269-283.

Buzan, B. (2001). The English School: an underexploited re source in IR. *Review of International Studies, 27*(03). https: //doi.org/10.1017/s0260210501004715

Buzan, B., & Lawson, G. (2017). *The English School: History and primary institutions as Empirical IR theory?* Oxford University Press.

Devlen, B., James, P., & Ozdamar, O. (2005). The English school, international relations, and Progress1. *Internation al Studies Review*, *7*(2), 171–197. https://doi.org/10.1111/j.1468-2486.2005.00480.x

Dunne, T., Kurki, M., & Smith, S. (Eds.). (2020). *International Relations Theories: Discipline and Diversity* (5th ed.). Oxford University Press.

Navari, C. (2013). World Society and English School Methods. *System, Society and School: Exploring the English School of International Relations*, 15-18. https://www.e-ir.info/2013/05/01/world-society-and-english-school-methods/

Suganami, H. (1983). The English school in a nutshell. *International Studies*, *2001*(2010b), 2004. http://www.ritsumei.ac.jp/ir/isaru/assets/file/raris/raris-09-02Hidemi_Suganami.pdf

CHAPTER 7

Social Constructivism

Lingkai Kong, Mahmut Akpınar

Introduction

In the seventh chapter, we will talk about the idea of social constructivism by reviewing the works that are listed below: Wendt (1992)'s *Anarchy is What States Make of it: The Social Construction of Power Politics*, Wendt (2013)'s *Social Theory of International Politics* and Hurd (1999)'s *Legitimacy and Authority in International Politics.*

Coercion, Self-interest, and Legitimacy

According to Wendt (2013), theories of international relations are founded on the link between actor, process, and social structure. Today, we will investigate how a constructionist view of structure affects agent and how agent shapes and forms structure intersubjectively. Hurd (1999) identifies three ways in which social structure impacts actor as "coercion, self-interest, and legitimacy" - three social controls, or three currencies of power, while Wendt (2013) demonstrates a comparable idea of three material aspects of international relations as "power, interest, and institutions."

Coercion is a relation of unequal physical power between actors, in which strong states may force weaker states to modify their conduct. The notion derives from Hobbes and is based on the state's physical and material power. Hurd (1999) argues that coercion is a very easy kind of social control that may lead to agent conflict and resentment.

Self-interest refers to the reality that an actor's compliance with a regulation is primarily motivated by their personal gain. The function of government, according to Hurd (1999), is to provide a platform where all players may trade and negotiate their interests, where the essential political act is assent to a contract. Per the Wendt (1992), the system is basically Lockean, emphasizing mutually acknowledged property rights and collaboration. Hurd (1999) separates "self-interest" and "the pursuit of individual interest" in particular. The former stresses an instrumentalist approach and views personal interest as the determining factor, while the latter emphasizes a "proper" pursuit of interest irrespective of irrelevant circumstances. In the latter circumstance, actors might base their choices on compulsion, self-interest, and legitimacy.

Formally, legitimacy is defined by Hurd (1999) as "the normative opinion of an agent that a rule or institution should be followed." The most effective instrument for long-term social control is legitimacy. A conviction in normative validity and an internal feeling of moral duty may encourage rule observance. This "belief" is subjective, not objective. It is the actor's view of the institution as a concept, which in turn shapes his "interests" and "action." The definition incorporates three essential concepts: notion, interest, and conduct. Hurd (1999) stresses that the basis for legitimacy is not always moral or even legal, but varies from individual to individual.

Process to Reconstitution

These three modes of engagement are not completely segregated from one another; rather, they are often blended, overlapped, and even allowed to develop. The connection between the actor and the structure may be one of coercion in the beginning, but as time goes on, the actor will discover methods to adapt that are in their own self-interest. Wendt (1992) discusses the process of constructing the identity of Europeans. It originally stems from egocentric motives; nevertheless, the act of collaborating has a tendency to reframe those reasons by reconstituting identities and interests in terms of new inter-subjective understandings and commitments.

In addition, Wendt (2013) makes reference to Mikhail Gorbachev's "New Thinking" philosophy. First, the Soviet Union shattered the consensus about identity commitment. Next, it performed a critical examination of outdated ideas about the self and the other. Finally, it altered the identities and interests of the other parties that had contributed to the maintenance of those systems of interaction. In this manner, Gorbachev placed the West in a situation in which it was required to establish a relationship with the Soviet Union, so creating a framework for a transition in both identity and interests. The transformation that took place in the Soviet

Union was not caused by structural pressures; rather, it was the consequence of a rebuilding of identity and interests. This demonstrates that the "reflective model" is more accurate than the "blind forces model." In the previous paragraph, we introduced the ideas of "interest," "identification," "reflective," "self-interest/egoistic," "inter-subjective," "power," "culture," "idea," "belief," "structure," and "actor," among other ideas. These ideas are essential to a complete comprehension of social constructivism and are thus crucial to all of us. Following that, we shall go on to the presentation of social constructivism and its activities in an official manner.

Social Constructivism

Hurd (1999) asserts that neoliberal and neorealist theories of society and power lie under the sphere of "coercion and self-interest." Also mentioned by Wendt (1992) is the disagreement between realists and liberals. He attributes the effect of state behavior to "structure" (anarchy and power distribution) and "process" (interaction and learning). Hurd (1999) then argues that legitimacy gets less attention than neorealism-coercion and neoliberalism-self-interest, and he equates social constructivism to the legitimacy analysis approach and emphasizes its need. He examines the writings of experts such as Bruce Russet and Michael Barnett and argues that none of them explain how legitimacy functions in the international system. The constructivism complements neorealism and contradicts the notion that crude materialism has no impact on international relations. Neoliberalism is complemented by the manner in which ideas build interests. The difference between "weak liberals" and "strong liberals" is made by Wendt (1992). The former admit the rhetorical and substantive causal capabilities of anarchy and accept rationalism's limitations, but "strong liberals" hold a key role in identity and interest shifts. Wendt argues, based on a solid liberal foundation, that constructivism stresses how informed activities produce subject. Constructivists share a cognitive, intersubjective view of process where identities and interests are endogenous to interaction. Wendt continues to add to learning and cognition, argues that self-help and power politics are also institutions, and refutes anarchic states.

The fundamental tenet of social constructivism is that individuals behave toward things, including other actors, based on their beliefs - meanings that they construct themselves. An essential characteristic of constructivism is holism or structuralism. As agents observe, recognize, and engage intersubjectively, they continually and collectively form institutions and cultures, while institutions re-constitute agents' interests and identities. Wendt (2013) argues that international politics is mostly determined by the distribution of interests, and produced by ideas.

Wendt (2013) distinguishes between desires and beliefs. Hume's assertion that desires usually include a combination of biological urges and beliefs, is an individual rather than a social matter. Constructivists need to transcend Hume's dualism and instead seek a cognitive theory that blends want and belief via "we want (desire) what we want because of how we think about it (belief)". Wendt (2013) also explains how international relations are created in terms of macro-micro views, causal and constitutive effects, and behavioral and properties perspectives. Interests are not defined by a set portfolio, but rather by an ongoing circumstance. Institutions are a collection of functions and structures for actors' collectively cognitive identities. Collective cognition and identities are mutually constitutive. Wendt (1992) describes institutionalization as the internalization of new identities and interests. He defines the "competitive" and "individualistic" security systems as "self-help" kinds of anarchy, as opposed to the state actively establishing its identity and interests. Thus, he suggests a "cooperative" security system in which identities and interests are intersubjectively constructed by states. Wendt (1992) then emphasizes that power politics is also socially created in everyday operations, but that does not imply that it is unreliable. Once a social system is established, each member is a social fact that promotes particular behaviors, and preserving the system's stability also supports individuals' stable role identification. Intersubjective understandings and expectations have this "self-perpetuating nature." Similarly, culture as an institution/system, is not only shared concept, but a "self-fulfilling prophecy" surviving the on-going public space development (Wendt, 2013).

Social Constructivism Practices of Sovereignty

For the practical implications of constructivism for IR, Hurd (1999) choose sovereignty as a tool and bases its construction on coercion, self-interest, and legitimacy, respectively. He argues that sovereignty is not an isolated idea, but rather a relative systemic concept of interaction. If there is just one state, there is no sovereignty. There are two main reasons why we emphasize sovereignty as a practice: 1. It is a basic idea in international relations upon which other talks are based. 2. Institutional sovereignty is seldom questioned (Hurd, 1999). Therefore, Wendt (1992) argues that sovereignty is a continual achievement of practice, whereas "practice is the core of constructivist resolutions to the agent-structure problem." The legitimacy institutions contradict the prevalent concept of anarchy, given that a state acknowledges certain international rules as legitimate and continuously shapes the system.

The mechanism of international governance is sovereignty, not international government. The lack of governance is not synonymous with anarchy. Bull (2012) acknowledges that the international order is not maintained by rules, but by creating the social milieu in which the rules work. Hurd (1999) demonstrates this in two different ways. 1. He proposes the existence of legitimacy for social control in the domestic context. 2. He directly looks for evidence of cases to prove the role of legitimacy.

Hurd (1999) mentions: 1. In sovereignty as coercion, states would use physical force to maintain borders such as Iraq and Iran. If there is a military imbalance, governments and territories will shift. But that doesn't happen. 2. The sovereignty-as-self-interest tenet of neoliberalism predicts that nations would continuously evaluate profits and losses. After calculating a favorable situation (to invade another state), the state conducts the plan. This also does not occur. 3. None of the aforementioned can explain the international system, but legitimacy does. State protection of boundaries and adherence to the international "law" of nonintervention derive from the legitimacy - "acceptable reach of state sovereign." Later, Wendt (2013) categorizes sovereign nations according to their beliefs/desires: status quo states, revisionist states, and collectivist states.

References

Bull, H. (2012). *The anarchical society: A study of order in world politics*. Palgrave Macmillan.

Hurd, I. (1999). Legitimacy and authority in international politics. *International Organization, 53*(2), 379–408. https://doi.org/10.1162/002081899550913

Wendt, A. (1992). Anarchy is what states make of it: the s ocial construction of power politics. *International Organi zation*, *46*(2), 391–425. https://doi.org/10.1017/s0020818300 027764

Wendt, A. (2013). *Cambridge studies in international relations: Social theory of international politics series number 67*. Cambridge University Press.

CHAPTER 8

Gender in International Relations

Mahmut Akpınar, Lingkai Kong

Introduction

In the eighth chapter, we will talk about the gender in international relations by reviewing the works that are listed below: Weber (1994)'s *Good Girls, Little Girls, and Bad Girls: Male Paranoia in Robert Keohane's Critique of Feminist International Relations,* Halliday (1988)'s *Hidden from International Relations: Women and the International Arena,* and Tickner (1997)'s *You Just Don't Understand: Troubled Engagements between Feminist and IR Theorists.*

Feminism in International Relations

Questions pertaining to gender, and more specifically the

position and function of women, have gained increased significance across the board in the field of social sciences over the course of the last two decades. There has been a discernible shift in the goals and ideas that are explored across a variety of academic fields as a direct response to the growth of a women's movement and the creation of a growing corpus of analytic literature that belongs to the women's viewpoint. Academic thinking is combined with the fact that the domain of international practice, in foreign ministries, ministries of defense, and related policy bodies, is itself an especially male-dominated, beyond even the norms common in policy-making bodies as a whole. According to the prevailing mindset, women are not equipped to handle obligations of this kind and cannot be relied upon in times of crisis or national security. It would seem that concerns about women and those regarding security couldn't be more different if they tried. There is, however, a more basic cause for the gender blindness that is prevalent across the majority of the study of international relations, and that reason is an assumption of separation between the two worlds of gender and international relations.

Therefore, the ideology known as feminism advocates for

the social, economic, and political equality of men and women. Despite having its origins primarily in the Western world, feminism can be found all over the globe and is represented by a broad variety of organizations that are dedicated to advocating for the rights and interests of women. Feminist theories, which are variously referred to as Marxist, radical, psychoanalytic, socialist, standpoint, existentialist, and postmodern, describe the causes and consequences of women's oppression and prescribe strategies for removing it.

An examination of gender dynamics provides a fresh angle on the study of international relations and poses a new group of problems. In the 1980s, early feminist international relations theorists joined other critical approaches to the field in questioning the traditional conceptual terrain of IR scholarship. These traditional concepts included states and sovereignty, national security, war, economic development and trade, and globalization. Other critical approaches to the field included: To better understand how social relations of masculinity and femininity, of gender identities and sexualities, and of gender difference are implicated in international politics, scholars who have focused their research on questions pertaining to gender and international relations have arrived at a consensus on a common statement. A necessary corrective to a field focused almost exclusively on the experiences of men and male-dominated institutions and practices, one of the tasks that feminist scholars in international relations have been tasked with is the establishment of a body of research on women. According to the findings of these researchers, the examination of gender as a method of social differentiation connected to power hierarchies reveals a landscape that is conceptually and empirically more complicated and distinct.

Feminist Empiricism, Standpoint and Postmodernism

Keohane examined feminist body of literature with reference to the three categories of feminism stated by Sandra Harding feminist empiricism, which in a general sense, refers to any epistemology that blends the technique of empiricists with the political aims of feminists. There is a school of thought among many feminists that empiricist methodologies are inherently incompatible with the achievement of feminist political aims. In this century, the term "empiricism" has become synonymous with "logical positivism." According to Harding, feminist empiricism may be traced back to one of the most basic assumptions of positivism (Campbell, 1994).

The second concept - the feminist standpoint refers to standpoint theory, which is a theoretical stance held by feminists that asserts that one's social position is the source of one's knowledge. This viewpoint rejects the idea that conventional science is objective and posits instead that research and theory have disregarded and excluded women as well as feminist modes of thinking for a very long time. The Marxist notion that persons belonging to an oppressed class have particular access to information that is not accessible to those belonging to a privileged class gave rise to the idea.

In the third concept, the feminist postmodernism theory, its main constituency can be referred to consist of those women (and men) who rely on its insights and the movement it articulates to orient their lives in more egalitarian and non-exploitative ways. These ways can be seen in sexual relations, the raising of children, the politics of the workplace, and domestic arrangements (Ebert, 1991).

"Good Girl", "Little Girl" and "Bad Girl"

The implications of Keohane's words on the three forms of feminism are distinct. In contrast to Harding and Sylvester, who view the world through a feminist lens, Keohane, in his view, takes as his object of analysis the three feminist categories "Good Girl", "Little Girl" and "Bad Girl" that define feminist ways of seeing, rather than using feminist perspectives to complement and transform his vision of international relations theory (Weber, 1994).

Good Girls: The feminist perspective is valued in Keohane's text owing to the perspective it gives to international relations theory. In the text, feminist perspective is described as a combined perspective that complements conventional International Relations. Keohane says that the feminist (standpoint) theorist critiques ideas developed by males who assume the role of policymakers. Feminists instead study international relations critically from the perspective of those who have been systemically excluded from power. In particular, the feminist perspective is described as requiring a reexamination of fundamental ideas such as power, sovereignty, and reciprocity. The feminist perspective does not stray from disciplinary objectives. Importantly, feminism is compatible with the rules of scientific inquiry. Keohane certainly has a feminist perspective with those who have a same critical objective and adhere to the standards of good science and support the discipline's aims, which include the gathering and evaluation of information about fundamental international relations topics. The disciplinary appearance of Keohane fetishizes a feminist perspective and additionally, Keohane discusses feminist institutionalism. The perspective of institutional feminism ceases to be an adjunct to the core of international relations theory and is integrated into the core itself. Therefore, the feminism no longer poses a danger to the core of international relations, since it has become an integral component of that core.

Little Girls: If feminist standpoint is a good girl in the science and discipline of international relations, then feminist empiricism is her younger sister. Keohane proposes that in examining how gender, the institutionalization of sex differences, influences the contemporary interstate system, feminist empiricism stresses that women have been victims of patriarchal governments and that both primary components of contemporary international relations - the institutionalization of war and the strengthening of state sovereignty - have had negative, and sometimes devastating, consequences on the lives of women. Feminist empiricism is more inclined to explain than to hypothesize. In contrast to the feminist viewpoint described in Keohane's work as a particularly promising starting place for the creation of feminist international relations theory, feminist empiricism seems to have a less developed view of international relations theory. In order for feminist empiricism to grow and attain a broader viewpoint, Keohane's text suggests that it form an alliance with its older sister, the feminist standpoint.

Bad Girls: Feminist postmodernism is defined as the feminist literature's dead end. It is the portion of the feminist body that has been removed in order for the other parts to survive. According to Keohane, this amputation is a necessary sacrifice on the part of the feminist body and the body of international relations theory in general, as it is the only disciplinary technique that can protect us to some extent from deflections such as nihilism and relativist resignation, which reinforce the status quo. Feminist postmodernism cannot be made to support scientific rules or the discipline's objectives, in contrast to feminist empiricism, it is not only a question of time until feminist postmodernism matures and becomes an integral part of international relations theory.

References

Campbell, R. (1994). The virtues of feminist empiricism. *Hy patia*, *9*(1), 90–115. https://doi.org/10.1111/j.1527-2001.1994. tb00111.x

Ebert, T. L. (1991). The "Difference" of Postmodern Feminism. *College English*, *53*(8), 886–904. https://doi.org/10.2307/377692

Halliday, F. (1988). Hidden from international relations: W omen and the international arena. *Millennium Journal of International Studies*, *17*(3), 419–428. https://doi.org/10.11 77/03058298880170030701

Tickner, J. A. (1997). You just don't understand: Troubled engagements between feminists and IR theorists. *Intern ational Studies Quarterly: A Publication of the Internationa l Studies Association*, *41*(4), 611–632. https://doi.org/10.111 1/1468-2478.00060

Weber, C. (1994). Good girls, little girls, and bad girls: Male paranoia in Robert keohane's critique of feminist international relations. *Millennium Journal of International Studies*, *23*(2), 337–349. https://doi.org/10.1177/03058298940230021401

CHAPTER 9

Marxist and Neo-Marxist Approaches in IR

Lingkai Kong, Mahmut Akpınar

Introduction

In the ninth chapter, we will talk about the Marxist and neo-Marxist approaches in international relations by reviewing the works that are listed below: Linklater (1986)'s *Realism, Marxism and Critical International Theory,* his *Marxism* in the book (2005) *Theories of International Relations,* and Cox (1983)'s *Gramsci, Hegemony and IR*. Linklater (1986, 2005) presents the fundamentals of Marxism and its approach to international relations, as well as the critical theory of Marxism's limitations in the social and IR fields. Cox (1983) discusses the application of Gramsci's hegemony theory to international relations comprehension.

Marxism and Its Criticism

Marxism, which emerged in the 1840s with Karl Marx and Friedrich Engels' social and economic debates stemming from the working class struggle, is expressed in international relations by the notion that capitalism globalization is "eroding the foundations of the international system of states" (Linklater, 2005). Marx not only contends that socialism will replace capitalism ineluctably, but also forecasts that this replacement of "alienation, exploitation, and estrangement" would occur globally. Conflicts between the two social classes, the national bourgeoisie and the cosmopolitan proletariat, would replace the antagonism between states. This has in fact two faces: the conflict between bourgeoisie and proletariat in the fundamental notion of Marxist political economy, and the contradiction between national and cosmopolitan space in the realm of international relations (Linklater, 2005).

Linklater (2005) asserts that some academics have criticized Marxist historical materialism for its excessive emphasis on the economic elements of human affairs in its analysis of international relations. Marxism views class struggle and political revolution as the "chief form" and "primary agent" for advancing historical development, technical innovation as the "driving-force" (Linklater, 2005), and human history primarily as the history of production. At a certain point in history, class structures restrict human freedom of action, yet people have the potential of "self-determination" to advance the historical process via class struggles. As production increases, communism will replace capitalism on a worldwide basis. Before actualization, Marxism effectively assimilates Hegel's concept of human appreciation for freedom and social awareness. The most influential Marxist account of globalization argues that "The bourgeoisie, by the rapid improvement of all instruments of production, by the immensely facilitated means of communication, draws all, even the most barbarian nations, into civilization" (Marx and Engels, 1977), in which the sense of "nationality" would be diminished in enlightened members of the proletariat, while humanity would still live in states divided along national lines and controlled by national bourgeoisie. Marxism holds that the proletariat must first gain power in its home nation before pursuing its worldwide objectives.

Marxism forecasts erroneously that capitalism is

"short-lived and that its inexorable laws would lead to its destruction" and disregards "the importance of the nation-state and violence in the contemporary world," or "renewed ethnic violence and national fragmentation." Marxism also fails to forecast the rise of nationalism as a result of globalization, and focuses excessively on the globalization of money rather than global security. And in essence, the traditional Marxist vision of liberation is founded on "a culture-bound view of the world that was inherited from the European Enlightenment" (Linklater, 2005), while excluding the non-European viewpoint. In a different study, Linklater (1986) argues that Marxism does not adequately explain how to create socialism, and that this lack of explanation and direction contributed to the Soviet Union's shift towards power politics.

Linklater (1986) says that the achievement of a critical theory entails resolving the clash between the ideals of this ethical tradition and the realities of political practice. In international theory, this term refers to "the resolution of this tension between principle and practice, resulting in the outline of an emancipatory practice." While Marxist theory has made a minor contribution to the aforementioned, it is recommended that social theory evolve beyond a Marxist viewpoint. To address Marxism's shortcomings, Frankfurt School researchers attempt to keep the "spirit" of traditional Marxism while diverging from its "letter." With "higher human knowledge," Habermas seeks to recreate historical materialism (Linklater, 2005). Robert Cox employs historical materialism to analyze social forces, governments, and international order, whereas the Neo-Gramscian school emphasizes global hegemony.

Gramsci's Theory of Hegemony

There are two roads leading to Gramsci's theory of hegemony: one from the Bolshevik revolution of proletariat hegemony, and the other from Machiavelli's attempts to build the state in a larger framework of "dominance and subordination" (Cox, 1983). Gramsci examines the disparity between the strength of civil society in Russia and Western Europe in his first approach. In Russia, where civil society is weaker, it would be very easy for a tiny minority to overturn the government and create a new regime via "wars of movement." In Western Europe, where the bourgeoisie is dominant and civil society is more established, the communist revolution involves "wars of position," which need the proletariat to gradually create the foundations of the societal revolution, disseminate influence, and acquire popular support (Cox, 1983).

Gramsci also discusses two distinct types of Western European societies. The first, including Britain and France, undergoes a profound social upheaval and the development of mature forms of production, with the industrial bourgeoisie seizing power. In the second, as in Italy, the industrial bourgeoisie does not attain hegemony, but the old dominating social groups and the new industrial bourgeoisie actively stagnate, causing a "passive revolution" in the nation. In Italy, the state becomes a union of the northern industrial bourgeoisie and the southern landowners, accompanied by two characteristics: Caesarism, which emphasizes the rule of a strong leader, and Trasformismo, which seeks to co-opt industrial interests with old dominant classes to prevent class-based social opposition (Cox, 1983).

Gramsci's theory of hegemony is well-suited to international relations, as the state is the primary actor in international conflict. Some nation-based revolutions may have an effect on other countries, consistent with the principle of passive influence discussed above. The notion that a tiny portion of the ruling class is formed from "an idealistic shaped ungroundedly in a domestic economic development" (Cox, 1983) corresponds with the criticism of traditional Marxism as "a culture-bound vision of the universe that was acquired from the European Enlightenment" (Linklater, 2005).

Gramsci refers to the segmentation of recent historical periods and the hegemonic status at certain points. During the period from 1845 and 1875, the United Kingdom is the economic hegemony of the globe. The second historical era, 1875-1945, is regarded as an unstable, non-hegemonic time. The period from 1945 and 1965 is characterized by the establishment of the new American hegemony. The author mentions the weakening of American hegemony throughout the fourth historical era, from 1965 to the present. According to Cox (1983), hegemony is a system of universal norms, institutions, and procedures that "lay down general rules of behaviour for states." Typically, the hegemonic state establishes international organizations and institutions, and hegemony has been acquired via social and economic revolutions, by spreading the economic, cultural, and technical institutions of one state to others. This dispersion from the center to the periphery constitutes a "passive revolution." In this growth process, the elites of peripheral nations are co-opted into international organizations in a Transformismo-like way. Negatively, they merely serve to sustain the ruling class's dominance and hegemony (Cox, 1983).

Similar to the class struggle in Western Europe, where the proletariat must establish its social basis in order to win "wars of position," the worldwide vision of counter-hegemony is similarly built on social relations. In times of economic distress, the reduction of transfer payments to low-income and working-class individuals builds the social foundation for change and revolution. For international communists, a more effective political organization that relies on the working class "generated by international production and building a bridge to peasants and urban marginals" is required, as without it, people can only live in a society ruled by elites who recklessly extend their power in a "monopoly-liberal world order."

References

Linklater, A., Burchill, S., & Devetak, R. (2005). *Theories of International Relations*. Palgrave Macmillan.

Cox, R. W. (1983). Gramsci, hegemony and international re lations : An essay in method. *Millennium Journal of Inte rnational Studies, 12*(2), 162–175. https://doi.org/10.1177/03058298830120020701

Engels, F., & Marx, K. (2015). *The communist manifesto*. Penguin Classics.

Linklater, A. (1986). Realism, Marxism and critical international theory. *Review of International Studies, 12*(4), 301–312. https://doi.org/10.1017/s0260210500113865

CHAPTER 10

Critical Approaches in IR

Mahmut Akpınar, Lingkai Kong

Introduction

In the last chapter, we will talk about some critical approaches in IR including globalization theory, post structuralism and orientalism by reviewing the works that are listed below: Dunne et al. (2016)'s *International Relations Theories: Discipline and Diversity,* Kinnvall (2004)'s *Globalization and Religious Nationalism: Self, Identity, and the Search for Ontological Security,* Michel (1980)'s *Truth and Power* and Said (2003)'s *Orientalism.*

Globalization

In the context of contemporary international relations,

globalization is one of the most dynamic, contentious, and debated problems. The process is open to a large variety of different definitions, but the vast majority of academics and observers believe that it constitutes a worldwide process of growing economic, cultural, and political interconnectedness and integration, with roots that go back very far in history. This is a process that has been promoted and managed to a greater or lesser degree by international institutions, multinational corporations, national governments, international nongovernmental organizations, and even individuals who have access to the Internet, a process that has been fed by liberalized international trade as well as innovations in information technology and communication.

The process of globalization has been going on for quite some time, and it has brought about significant shifts in terms of "scale," "speed," and "cognition." When seen on a global basis, the scale of economic, political, and social links that exist between nations and cultures is more than it has ever been before throughout the course of human history. In terms of speed, globalization includes a compression of time and space that has never before been experienced. In terms of cognition, there is an increased perception of the globe as a smaller place, which means that events elsewhere have results for our everyday political, social, and economic lives, which in turn affects individuals' sense of being. In many regions of the globe, the expansion of democratic principles has further contributed to the social dislocation that exists there. Norms of equality and "egalitarianism" have a tendency to undermine the legitimacy of preexisting hierarchical systems. As conventional power relations have become more democratic, long-established behavioral patterns have been rendered less reliable as a result. The structures that recognized the community and linked it together are also being erased, which has the effect of disintegrating the community. These findings point to the strong relationship that globalization has with security, and further evidence may be seen in the way in which migrants, asylum seekers, and refugees are now portrayed in terms of security risks.

The "Thick Signifier" is the first idea that has to be presented to the viewer: A thick signifier approach focuses on the contextual aspects of security, as it mentions a search for key dimensions of the wider order of meaning within which the framework itself is established. The purpose of a thick signifier analysis is to comprehend how a certain metaphysics of existence is implied by security jargon. The interpretation does not just explain how a security narrative involves the characterization of dangers, a referent object, etc.; rather, it explains how it defines our interactions to nature, to other human beings, and to ourselves. Therefore, security as a thick signifier locates a person or group within the larger discursive and institutional continuities in which they are entrenched. This may apply to both individuals and groups. Unmasking the structural linkages that serve as the framework for security discourses is required in order to take a thick signifier approach to the concept of security. These structural relations are a reflection of the division that exists between those who are engaged and impacted by the oration as well as the disparity of power that exists between them. Those who generate the oration also have the authority to make it "true," or to impose a specific interpretation of a danger according to which persons and groups are defined.

"Ontological Security and Existential Anxiety" is the second idea that plays a significant part in global affairs. According to Giddens, ontological security refers to a person's fundamental feeling that they are secure in the world and incorporates a fundamental confidence in the people around them. Obtaining such trust becomes vital for a person to keep up a feeling of psychological well-being and to avoid existential anxiety in order for the individual to be able to avoid existential anxiety. To put it another way, ontological security might be described as a feeling of certainty and faith that the world is exactly as it seems to be. It's a security of being. Trusting other people is like to receiving an emotional vaccination against existential fears. It is a protection against future threat and danger, which enables a person to maintain hope and bravery in the face of any harrowing conditions that they may later be forced to face.

In such interpretations, the prevalence of religion and nationalism may thus drive the creation of new local identities as a reaction to the destabilizing impacts of globalization. It is at times like these, when people are without a place to call home and feel alone, that leaders may seem to reflect existential worries as well as sentiments of loss and despair. The opposition to and rejection of established power structures are encouraged by the globalization of the local, often known as the link between global and local issues. The development and rebuilding of historical symbols, myths, and selected traumas provide alternate beliefs to the day-to-day uneasiness that people experience. The more inclusive a set of beliefs is, the more likely it is that it will be exclusive to persons or groups who aren't included in the definition of those views. Consequently, the creation of the self and the other is virtually always used as a means to define more superior and less superior individuals. Those who are on the inside (of the religion or country) are superior because they symbolize purity, order, truth, beauty, good, and right, while those who are on the outside are impacted by pollution, falsehood, ugliness, evil, and wrong.

Post structuralism

In the 1980s, post-structuralism made its debut in international relations thanks to the contributions of scholars such as Richard Ashley, James Der Derian, Michael Shapiro, and R. B. J. Walker. Early research were compiled in two significant collections: Der Derian and Shapiro (1989) and Ashley and Walker (1990). These focused primarily on states and the meta-theoretical critique of realist and neorealist theories to indicate how the theoretical assumptions of the traditional perspectives shaped what could be said about international politics. Critical academics were unsatisfied with the way realism remained dominant in the face of new global developments, as well as its revivification at that time via neorealism. According to some academics, realism downplayed the significance of new transnational actors, concerns, and linkages and neglected to acknowledge or even listen to the voices of excluded peoples and viewpoints. As a result, the origins of post-structuralism may be traced back to an ethical concern to include those who had been ignored or left out by the "mainstream". When discussing how the links between the inner and the outside were mutually produced, the post-structural perspectives were brought up. In the sake of realism, the state drew a line between "inside" and "outside," sovereign" and "anarchic, "we" and "them." As a result, post-structuralism started out by asking why the state was seen to be the most significant player in international politics, as well as why the state was considered to be a "unitary, rational actor." Because of this, one of the primary concerns of post-structuralism from the onset was the practices of statecraft that gave the impression that the state and its significance were both natural and unavoidable. This approach is neither "anti-state," nor does it strive to get beyond the state, nor does it neglect the state. Poststructuralism is more attentive to the state than realism is. This is due to the fact that post-structuralism is concerned with the state's historical and conceptual production, as well as its political formation, economic constitution, and social exclusions, whereas realism only defends that the state is the foundation of its paradigm.

Orientalism

The Orient is an intrinsic component of European material culture and civilization. Orientalism defines and expresses that portion culturally and even ideologically as a way of mentioning with supporting institutions, lexicon, research, images, ideologies, and even colonial bureaucracy and colonial fashions. Orientalist theory is founded on an ontological and epistemic dichotomy between the Orient and the Occident. Historiographically and culturally, there is a quantitative and qualitative contrast between the Franco-British focus on the Orient and the engagement of every other European and Atlantic power prior to the time of American dominance following World War II.

It would be erroneous to assume that the Orient is primarily a concept or a fabrication devoid of matching reality. According to Claimed, when Disraeli said in his book *Tancred* that the East was a profession, he meant that intelligent young Westerners would find an interest in the East to be an all-consuming passion; he did not imply that the East was a job just for Westerners. There have been and continue to be civilizations and countries whose location is in the East, and whose lives, history, and traditions are manifestly more genuine than anything the West might say about them. About this reality, this study of Orientalism contributes very nothing, except to accept it implicitly. A second condition is that ideas, cultures, and histories cannot be researched or comprehended properly without also studying their force, or more precisely, their power arrangements. The relationship between the Occident and the Orient is one of power, dominance, and varying degrees of a complex hegemony. It is hypocritical to believe that the Orient was created or, as he calls it, "Orientalized," and to believe that such things occur solely due to the necessity of the imagination. The final condition is that Orientalism is not a European fantasy about the Orient, but rather a developed corpus of thought and practice in which significant material investment has been made over many generations. Continued investment made Orientalism, as a system of knowledge about the Orient, an acceptable grid for filtering the Orient into Western awareness, just as it expanded the claims emanating from Orientalism into the wider culture.

According to Said, the strategy of Orientalism is dependent on flexible positional supremacy, which places the Westerner in an infinite number of conceivable interactions with the Orient without ever relinquishing his relative advantage. Moreover, he asks, "why should it have been different, particularly throughout the unprecedented era of European hegemony from the late Renaissance to the present?" The scientist, the scholar, the missionary, the merchant, and the soldier were in or contemplated the Orient because they were able to be there or contemplate it with little opposition from the Orient.

References

Ashley, R. K., & Walker, R. B. J. (1990). Conclusion: Reading Dissidence/Writing the Discipline: Crisis and the Question of Sovereignty in International Studies. *International Studies Quarterly*, *34*(3), 367–416. https://doi.org/10.2307/2600576

Der Derian, J., & Shapiro, M. J. (Eds.). (1989). *International/intertextual relations: postmodern readings of world politics*. Lexington Books.

Dunne, T., Kurki, M., & Smith, S. (Eds.). (2020). *International Relations Theories: Discipline and Diversity* (5th ed.). Oxford University Press.

Foucault, M., & Gordon, C. (1977). *Truth and Power In Power/Knowledge: Selected Interviews and Other Writings*. Pantheon.

Kinnvall, C. (2004). Globalization and religious nationalism: Self, identity, and the search for ontological securit y. *Political Psychology*, *25*(5), 741–767. https://doi.org/10.1111/j.1467-9221.2004.00396.x

Said, E. W. (2003). *Orientalism*. Penguin Classics.

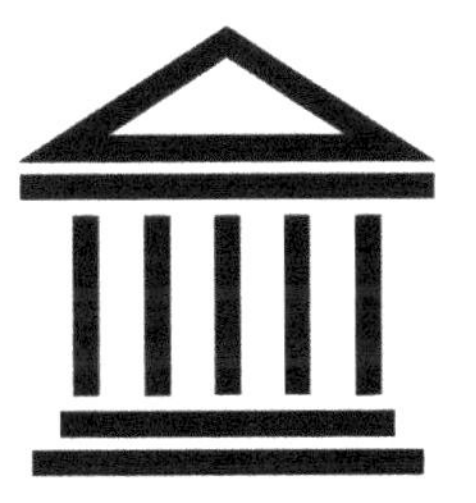

IIOPS

Istanbul Institute of
Political Strategy

www.ingramcontent.com/pod-product-compliance
Ingram Content Group UK Ltd.
Pitfield, Milton Keynes, MK11 3LW, UK
UKHW020418250726
13967UKWH00007B/2710

9 781739 271206